Tech Terms For Trustees

Decoding I.T. Terms For Hospital Boards

Clear & To The Point
Book 2

Ron Galloway

Contents

Foreword

I often give talks at healthcare conferences, many times with C-suite level staff and hospital trustees.

Sometimes when I mention certain technical terms (like FHIR), I see blank faces. Nice faces, but blank. The purpose of this book is to correct that.

Hospitals are now data institutions. And as such, the people charged with leadership of the hospital should have at least a passing understanding of the issues that will be presented before them in board meetings.

The hospital in my hometown was built in 1973 for an inflation adjusted cost of $175 million. The cost for that hospital's electronic healthcare records system was $185 million.

So the system managing the data for the patients cost more than the infrastructure that houses the institution!

Today, it's incumbent on trustees to familiarize themselves with general terms surrounding data, at least where it regards healthcare.

Foreword

Hopefully this book will help. It is meant as a useful, targeted reference, and I believe it is best dipped into from time to time to learn new concepts.

I also hope it's a good tool to skim over before a board meeting involving technology. For instance, if you know there's going to be a discussion of electronic healthcare records on the agenda, this book might help demystify some of the terms you will doubtless hear.

Chapter 1
Application Programming Interfaces (APIs)
The Invisible Backbone of Digital Healthcare

If you're serving on a hospital board, you've likely heard the term "API" thrown around in IT meetings. It sounds technical, and it is, but the concept is straightforward. APIs, or Application Programming Interfaces, are how digital systems communicate with one another without needing human involvement.

Think of an API as a digital handshake. Two systems, say, a lab database and an electronic health record (EHR), need to share data. An API enables that exchange instantly and securely, without requiring someone to manually transfer files or re-enter data.

Hospitals are built on dozens of siloed systems: radiology archives, appointment schedulers, billing engines, pharmacy platforms, and more. APIs are what tie those systems together, enabling real-time functionality across departments and vendors. Without APIs, your digital tools remain isolated. With APIs, your infrastructure becomes dynamic and responsive.

Core Mechanisms Behind APIs

Here's how APIs actually function inside a healthcare environment:

- **RESTful APIs:** These are the workhorses of web-based communication. They use standard web protocols like GET, POST, PUT, and DELETE to retrieve or update information. RESTful APIs are stateless, which makes them scalable across large health systems. Example: A patient portal pulls lab results from an EHR using a RESTful API, without exposing the entire medical record.
- **FHIR (Fast Healthcare Interoperability Resources):** This is the healthcare-specific language of APIs. It ensures that data from different systems is structured in the same way, so machines can understand it. Example: A FHIR-enabled system knows that a medication list or allergy report has the same format across providers, making data portable and consistent.
- **OAuth 2.0:** This is the security layer that ensures only authorized parties can access sensitive data. It enables third-party apps to access a patient's health information, only after receiving consent. Example: A fitness app reads EHR data only after the patient gives explicit permission through a secure authentication process.

Where APIs Are Making an Impact

You don't need to understand the code, but you do need to understand the capability. APIs are behind nearly every digital innovation hospitals pursue today.

- **Real-Time Data Exchange:** When a patient is transferred, APIs make sure their chart arrives before they do. Example: A discharge summary from one facility is instantly available to the admitting physician at another.
- **Patient Engagement:** APIs allow EHR data to flow into mobile health apps and dashboards that patients actually use. Example: A hypertension app shows how lifestyle changes are affecting blood pressure, because the app is pulling data via API.
- **Clinical Innovation:** AI tools, clinical decision support systems, and diagnostic platforms all require structured, fast access to data. Example: An AI triage tool scans EHR data to help prioritize ER cases, relying entirely on real-time API data flow.
- **Operational Efficiency:** APIs automate previously manual tasks. Example: Appointment systems sync calendars, billing platforms verify insurance, and supply chain software tracks inventory, with no manual data entry.

Why This Matters for Trustees

APIs aren't a tech feature. They're the infrastructure beneath innovation.

They allow your hospital to compete, by reducing friction, enabling partnerships, and supporting next-generation tools. Without APIs, integrating new platforms or complying with federal interoperability mandates becomes a logistical nightmare.

When regulators talk about the 21st Century Cures Act and data sharing, they're really talking about APIs. So when your IT team recommends "expanding API access," you're not just nodding, you understand exactly why it matters.

APIs aren't about software. They're about whether your hospital's systems, staff, and patients are flying blind, or fully connected.

Quiz Question

Which of the following is not a direct function of health-care APIs?

- A. Enabling in-person consultations with doctors
- B. Exchanging health records across systems
- C. Allowing secure access for third-party apps
- D. Supporting development of new digital tools

Correct Answer: A

APIs handle data exchange, not face-to-face care. Human interaction is still a core part of medicine.

Chapter 2
Ambient Clinical Intelligence

Listening in to Lighten the Clinical Load

Ambient Clinical Intelligence (ACI) refers to a suite of technologies, primarily voice recognition, natural language processing (NLP), and machine learning, that work quietly in the background to document clinical encounters and streamline workflows. It operates passively, capturing data from provider-patient interactions in real time, without requiring manual input or disruption.

ACI transforms the exam room into a low-friction, data-rich environment, allowing clinicians to focus on the patient, not the screen. It's not just a transcription tool, it's a new model for clinical efficiency and cognitive offloading.

Core Mechanisms Behind Ambient Clinical Intelligence

ACI systems function through the convergence of several advanced technologies:

- **Voice Recognition and NLP:** Transcribes spoken language and structures it into medical concepts and EHR-ready formats. Example: During an exam, ACI captures "The patient reports shortness of breath" and automatically logs it as a symptom in the EHR.
- **Contextual Awareness:** Learns the clinical setting and intent behind spoken phrases. Example: Recognizes that "Let's try a beta blocker" means a medication order and drafts the relevant order in the system.
- **Machine Learning and Workflow Integration:** Continuously improves accuracy and integrates seamlessly with clinical systems. Example: An ACI system learns each clinician's preferences and adjusts documentation formats or templates accordingly.

Transformative Applications in Healthcare

ACI supports frontline care delivery and administrative efficiency simultaneously.

- **Real-Time Clinical Documentation:** Eliminates after-hours charting and note-writing. Example: ACI records the encounter and generates structured progress notes while the clinician interacts naturally with the patient.
- **Reduced Cognitive Burden:** Lets clinicians focus on care, not computers. Example: A physician discusses symptoms and treatment options aloud while ACI handles the documentation and formulates next steps in the background.
- **Enhanced Patient Experience:** More eye contact, less typing. Example: ACI removes the barrier of a screen between doctor and patient, improving rapport and communication.
- **Streamlined EHR Interaction:** Cuts the time spent clicking and typing. Example: Orders, referrals, and follow-up instructions are auto-drafted from spoken commands and finalized with one tap.

Why This Matters for Trustees

Ambient Clinical Intelligence speaks directly to clinician burnout, patient satisfaction, and EHR usability, three pressure points facing every health system.

Trustees should ask: Are our clinicians spending more time documenting than treating? Is documentation quality improving or degrading under stress? Are we evaluating

ACI vendors with a focus on workflow impact, not just novelty?

ACI is not just a tool, it's a rethinking of how clinical data is captured and used. It offers the promise of higher accuracy, more human-centered care, and reduced administrative overhead.

Quiz Question

Which of the following is NOT a primary function of Ambient Clinical Intelligence in healthcare?

- A. Automatically transcribing clinical conversations into structured medical notes
- B. Ordering diagnostic tests and procedures without physician involvement
- C. Reducing clinician documentation burden through voice and context-aware systems
- D. Enhancing patient-provider communication by minimizing screen time

Correct Answer: B

ACI assists with documentation and order entry, but final clinical decisions and approvals still require human oversight.

Chapter 3
Artificial Intelligence
What It Really Means for Hospitals

AI gets thrown around like a buzzword, but for trustees, it needs grounding. At its core, artificial intelligence is about teaching machines to mimic human thinking, recognizing patterns, making decisions, understanding language, and even interpreting images.

In healthcare, AI is not some future dream. It's already shaping how care is delivered, how hospitals operate, and how patients experience the system.

AI isn't replacing doctors. It's giving them better tools.

Core Mechanisms Behind AI

Let's strip it down to four things your hospital is either already using, or will be soon:

- **Machine Learning (ML):** The engine behind AI. It trains computers to learn from past data. These algorithms can spot trends, make predictions, and improve over time. Example: An ML system flags patients most likely to be readmitted, helping staff intervene early.

- **Natural Language Processing (NLP):** This allows computers to understand and use human language. It powers everything from chatbots to clinical documentation. Example: A virtual assistant that lets patients reschedule an MRI by simply texting it in.
- **Robotics:** Not walking androids, but machines that assist with precision. Often used in surgery. Example: A robotic system that helps a surgeon perform delicate procedures with enhanced steadiness and control.
- **Computer Vision:** This is how AI sees, analyzing X-rays, CTs, MRIs, and other images. Example: A tool that scans mammograms and flags potential tumors for the radiologist to review.

Where It's Being Used in Healthcare

AI isn't magic. But when used right, it cuts through complexity.

- **Diagnostic Support:** AI tools can review thousands of images in minutes, flagging early signs of disease. They never get tired, and their suggestions give physicians a second set of eyes. Example: Retinal scans analyzed by AI to catch diabetic eye disease before symptoms appear.

- **Personalized Treatment:** Instead of using one-size-fits-all protocols, AI systems can tailor care to the individual. Their recommendations can take into account a patient's genetics, history, and risk factors. Example: Oncology platforms that generate specific treatment plans based on the molecular profile of a tumor.
- **Operational Efficiency:** AI can forecast staffing needs, detect billing errors, and reduce scheduling conflicts. That's not just administrative, it affects patient care. Example: A scheduling system that reallocates resources dynamically during flu season.
- **Public Health Prediction:** With access to population-level data, AI can spot disease trends before they hit the evening news. Example: Tracking ER visits and symptom clusters to predict a COVID surge two weeks ahead.

Why This Matters for Trustees

AI isn't optional. It's infrastructure.

Hospitals without an AI strategy will fall behind in both care quality and operational performance. And the use of AI isn't just for the academic medical centers anymore. Commercial systems are increasingly available off the shelf.

But oversight matters. Trustees need to know what tools are being used, how decisions are being made, and how patient data is handled. AI must be explainable, ethical, and aligned with your hospital's mission.

You don't need to understand the math. But you do need to ask: What problem is this solving? How is it measured? Who is accountable?

AI is a tool. And in healthcare, the right tool in the right hands saves lives.

Quiz Question

    A. Which of the following best describes the role of AI in healthcare?
    B. Replacing human healthcare professionals entirely
    C. Providing diagnostic support and personalizing treatment plans
    D. Solely improving the efficiency of hospital administrative tasks
    E. Only being used for robotic surgeries

Correct Answer: B

AI supports doctors. It doesn't replace them. It enhances diagnosis and personalizes care.

Chapter 4
Augmented Reality
**Making Healthcare Information
Tangible**

Augmented Reality (AR) blends digital information with the real world. In healthcare, it allows providers and patients to see anatomy, data, or procedures overlaid on physical space in real time.

This isn't virtual reality, it doesn't replace the real world. It enhances it.

With AR, healthcare becomes more interactive, more precise, and more engaging.

Core Mechanisms Behind Augmented Reality

AR brings value to healthcare through three main functions:

- **Image Overlay and Visualization:** Digital models placed on or within the real-world view. Example: A surgeon sees a 3D model of a patient's spine projected over the body during an operation.

- **Interactive Training and Education:** Complex concepts come to life. Example: Medical students use AR to explore 3D organ structures from every angle.
- **Real-time Information Display:** Key data is visible without breaking focus. Example: A doctor wearing AR glasses sees a patient's vitals and medical history during a physical exam.

Transformative Applications in Healthcare

AR supports both technical precision and human connection in care.

- **Improving Surgical Precision:** Visual data layered over anatomy during procedures. Example: An AR-assisted laparoscopic surgery system shows real-time imaging to guide instrument movement.
- **Enhancing Medical Training and Education:** Immersive learning replaces static models. Example: AR simulates trauma scenarios for emergency response training.
- **Facilitating Patient Care and Rehabilitation:** Engaging therapies improve compliance. Example: Patients recovering from strokes play AR games that guide hand movements and track progress.

- **Boosting Patient Understanding and Engagement:** Complex ideas become visual and personal. Example: An AR app shows a patient how a stent works inside their artery, easing pre-surgery anxiety.

Why This Matters for Trustees

AR is not science fiction. It's already reducing surgical errors and improving medical education. Trustees should consider how AR tools are integrated into care settings, how they're evaluated, and whether they align with clinical goals.

AR adds depth and clarity, turning data into action and understanding.

Quiz Question

Which of the following is NOT a typical use of AR in healthcare?

A. Automatically performing surgeries without human intervention
B. Assisting surgeons with real-time visualizations during procedures
C. Enhancing medical education through interactive 3D models
D. Supporting patient rehabilitation with engaging exercise programs

Correct Answer: A

AR enhances what surgeons see and do, it doesn't replace them. Surgery still requires skilled human hands.

Chapter 5
Big Data
Why It's Reshaping Modern Healthcare

Hospitals produce more data than almost any other organization. Every scan, every lab result, every patient history note, each one adds to the pile. This mountain of information is what we call Big Data.

But data alone doesn't change anything. What matters is how it's used.

When analyzed correctly, Big Data can spot problems earlier, streamline operations, personalize treatments, and even drive breakthrough research. It turns raw information into action.

Core Mechanisms Behind Big Data

Here's how hospitals are starting to harness all that data:

- **Data Analytics:** This is the engine. Analytics comb through millions of records to find patterns. Example: Analysts study thousands of patient files to identify who's most likely to develop Type 2 diabetes, and why.

- **Machine Learning and AI:** These systems don't just look at past data, they learn from it. Example: A model is trained on historical cases to predict how a specific patient might respond to a drug.
- **Data Visualization:** This turns numbers into something you can actually understand. Example: A dashboard shows infection rates by hospital wing in real time, guiding resource allocation.

Transformative Applications in Healthcare

Big Data isn't just for academics or IT departments. It's changing what's possible in care delivery and decision-making.

- **Predictive Analytics for Patient Care:** By spotting patterns across populations, providers can intervene before conditions worsen. Example: Algorithms flag heart failure risk based on vital signs, lab data, and lifestyle factors.
- **Patient Engagement and Outcomes:** The more data patients generate, via wearables or apps, the more tailored their feedback becomes. Example: A smartwatch tracks sleep and

activity, then recommends adjustments that align with the patient's cardiac rehab plan.

- **Operational Efficiency:** Hospitals can optimize everything from staffing to supply chains using historical data. Example: Peak ER admission times are analyzed to adjust shift coverage, reducing wait times.
- **Medical Research:** Researchers can tap massive datasets to uncover disease mechanisms and test hypotheses faster. Example: Millions of genomic records help pinpoint mutations linked to rare cancers, guiding drug development.

Why This Matters for Trustees

Big Data isn't a side project. It's a strategic asset.

Hospitals that use data well reduce costs, improve care quality, and make better decisions. Those that don't fall behind, not just in performance, but in compliance and innovation.

Trustees don't need to know how to code. But they do need to ask how data is being used. Who owns it? Who governs it? Is it actionable? And is it being used ethically?

Because with Big Data, the upside is enormous, but so is the responsibility.

Used right, Big Data won't just change how hospitals run. It'll change how medicine is practiced.

Quiz Question

Which of the following is NOT an application of Big Data in healthcare?

A. Automatically diagnosing patients without the review of a medical professional
B. Identifying public health trends through the analysis of population health data
C. Personalizing treatment plans based on analysis of a patient's genetic information
D. Improving hospital operational efficiency through predictive analytics

Correct Answer: A

Big Data helps inform diagnoses, but it doesn't replace clinical judgment.

Chapter 6
Biometrics
**Making Healthcare More Secure,
Personal, and Precise**

In healthcare, knowing who a person is, and verifying it with certainty, can be the difference between safety and error. That's where biometrics come in.

Biometrics are measurable traits, like your fingerprint, your face, or your voice, that can be used to identify you. These traits are unique, hard to fake, and increasingly easy to scan.

In a hospital setting, biometrics aren't just about convenience. They're about preventing wrong-patient procedures, securing sensitive data, and enabling personalized care without friction.

Core Mechanisms Behind Biometrics

Biometric systems typically fall into three categories, all with increasing relevance to modern hospitals.

- **Physiological Biometrics:** These include physical traits, fingerprints, facial geometry, iris scans. Example: A nurse uses a fingerprint to access the EHR system, ensuring secure, auditable access to patient records.
- **Behavioral Biometrics:** These are based on how someone moves or speaks. Example: A telehealth platform uses voice recognition to authenticate the patient before beginning a remote consult.
- **Wearable Biometric Sensors:** These continuously collect health data, like heart rate or blood glucose levels. Example: A smartwatch tracks a patient's heart rate variability to detect early signs of cardiac stress.

Transformative Applications in Healthcare

Biometrics aren't just about tighter security. They also improve patient safety and care delivery.

- **Enhanced Patient Identification:** Prevents mix-ups, especially in fast-paced clinical environments. Example: Facial recognition at the bedside ensures the right patient is receiving the right medication.
- **Improved Healthcare Security:** Protects restricted areas and sensitive systems without relying on passwords or keycards. Example: An

iris scan system controls access to a high-security medication storage area.

- **Personalized Monitoring:** Wearable devices provide real-time data that enables proactive interventions. Example: A wearable alerts a patient and provider when heart rate patterns deviate from baseline.
- **Remote Authentication:** Validates a patient's identity during virtual visits. Example: A telehealth app uses voiceprint recognition to verify the patient before sharing private health information.

Why This Matters for Trustees

Biometrics solve a problem that's only growing: too many patients, too many systems, too many risks.

As digital health expands, so do vulnerabilities, data breaches, identity mismatches, security gaps. Biometrics harden defenses while making workflows more efficient.

Trustees need to ensure that biometric systems are accurate, unbiased, and ethically deployed. They also need to know where the data is stored, who has access, and how it's used.

Done well, biometrics don't just improve security. They build trust, between patient and provider, system and user.

Quiz Question

Which of the following is NOT an application of biometrics in healthcare?

    A. Using gait analysis to determine a person's unique identity for secure access to online health records

    B. Implementing DNA sequencing as a standard method for patient login to hospital Wi-Fi networks

    C. Employing wearable devices to monitor and report changes in physiological parameters

    D. Utilizing fingerprint scans for patient identification and access to their electronic health records

Correct Answer: B

DNA sequencing is not used for routine biometric access. It's neither practical nor necessary for tasks like logging into a network.

Chapter 7
Blockchain
Rebuilding Trust in Healthcare Data

Blockchain may sound like it belongs in finance, but it's gaining serious ground in healthcare. Why? Because the problems it solves, data security, privacy, and trust, are exactly the ones hospitals face every day.

At its core, blockchain is a digital ledger. But instead of being stored in one place, it's spread across many computers. Once something is written into that ledger, it's nearly impossible to alter or delete.

This makes it ideal for a healthcare system drowning in fragmented records, fraud risk, and privacy concerns.

Core Mechanisms Behind Blockchain

Here are the building blocks that make blockchain work in a healthcare setting:

- **Decentralization:** There's no single owner of the data. It's stored across a distributed network. Example: A patient's record isn't housed in just one hospital, it's replicated across a blockchain network, accessible when needed but controlled by the patient.

- **Immutability:** Once entered, data cannot be tampered with. Example: A prescription entered into a blockchain can't be modified later, reducing the risk of fraud or error.
- **Smart Contracts:** These are self-executing agreements built into the code. Example: An insurance claim that meets all criteria gets approved instantly, no paperwork, no delays.

Transformative Applications in Healthcare

Blockchain isn't replacing EHRs or insurance systems. It's making them safer, faster, and more interoperable.

- **Secure Patient Data Management:** Patients can finally control access to their own medical records. Example: A blockchain-based portal lets patients authorize or revoke access to their data with a click.
- **Supply Chain Transparency:** Drugs and devices can be tracked from origin to destination, fighting counterfeits. Example: Each stage of a medication's journey, from manufacturing to pharmacy shelf, is logged and verified.

- **Interoperability and Data Exchange:**
  Disparate systems become part of one trusted
  network. Example: A decentralized data-
  sharing layer connects hospitals, clinics, and
  specialists without needing a central authority.
- **Clinical Trials and Research Integrity:** Data is
  time-stamped, consent is recorded, and results
  are verified. Example: A trial logs patient
  consent and data uploads in real time, ensuring
  compliance and protecting participant
  anonymity.

Why This Matters for Trustees

Trust in healthcare data is eroding. Patients don't know
who has their records. Providers struggle to share information. Insurers fight fraud. Blockchain addresses all of it.

But it's not plug-and-play. Trustees must understand
the implications: who maintains the network, how data
access is controlled, and what regulatory standards apply.

Done right, blockchain won't just modernize health IT,
it will restore confidence in the data itself.

Quiz Question

Which of the following is NOT a potential benefit of blockchain technology in healthcare?

- A. Centralizing patient data under a single healthcare provider
- B. Enhancing the security and privacy of patient health records
- C. Improving the traceability of pharmaceuticals and medical supplies
- D. Enabling secure and efficient health information exchange

Correct Answer: A

Blockchain decentralizes data, it doesn't centralize it under one authority.

Chapter 8

Chatbots

The Front Line of AI in Patient Communication

When patients ask simple questions, about symptoms, appointments, or prescriptions, they don't always need a human on the other end. That's where chatbots come in.

Healthcare chatbots are AI-powered tools that hold conversations via text or voice. They're available 24/7, never get tired, and can handle thousands of interactions at once.

They don't replace doctors. But they free up doctors to focus on what only they can do.

Core Mechanisms Behind Chatbots

Chatbots work because of three integrated technologies:

- **Natural Language Processing (NLP):** This allows the bot to understand and generate human-like conversation. Example: A chatbot asks follow-up questions about a patient's symptoms, then offers advice on whether to self-monitor or seek care.

- **Machine Learning (ML):** Chatbots improve as they gather more data from users. Example: A mental health chatbot adjusts its tone and responses based on previous conversations with a user.
- **Integration with Healthcare Systems:** Bots can pull information directly from EHRs or scheduling tools. Example: Before booking an appointment, a chatbot reviews the patient's history and recommends the right specialist.

Transformative Applications in Healthcare

Chatbots are already embedded in patient care pathways. Their uses are growing fast.

- **Improving Access to Information:** Chatbots respond instantly, anytime. Example: A symptom-checker bot triages users based on input and guides them to the appropriate next step.
- **Enhancing Patient Engagement:** Bots create a sense of continuity and accountability. Example: A chatbot reminds a diabetic patient to log their glucose levels and encourages consistent medication use.
- **Streamlining Healthcare Services:** Administrative overhead is reduced through

automation. Example: A bot books appointments, checks physician availability, and sends reminders, all without human intervention.

- **Supporting Mental Health:** Bots offer private, stigma-free environments for support. Example: A chatbot delivers CBT-based exercises to help a user navigate anxiety in real time.

Why This Matters for Trustees

Chatbots are low-cost, scalable, and already popular with patients. For health systems, they improve efficiency without compromising care quality.

But quality control matters. Trustees should ask: Who built the bot? What content does it serve? How is patient data protected? Chatbots must be transparent, secure, and aligned with clinical guidelines.

Done well, chatbots aren't gimmicks. They're digital front doors to care.

Quiz Question

Which of the following is NOT a typical function of healthcare chatbots?

- A. Conducting surgical procedures via robotic arms controlled by the chatbot
- B. Providing users with health information and answering their inquiries
- C. Reminding patients to take their medications at prescribed times
- D. Assisting with the scheduling of medical appointments

Correct Answer: A

Chatbots handle communication, not surgery. That's still the job of trained professionals.

Chapter 9
Clinical Decision Support Systems
Quietly Guiding Better Care

Behind every confident diagnosis or precise prescription, there's a growing chance a system played a supporting role. Clinical Decision Support Systems (CDSS) don't make decisions for doctors, but they make good decisions easier to reach.

These systems sit inside EHRs or hospital IT infrastructure and quietly scan patient data. When something looks off, or when something could be improved, they speak up.

They don't replace clinical judgment. They sharpen it.

Core Mechanisms Behind CDSS

CDSS tools rely on a blend of rules, algorithms, and unstructured data processing:

- **Rule-Based Systems:** These follow pre-defined if-then logic. Example: If a patient's on blood

thinners, and a new drug creates a bleeding risk, the system sends an alert.
- **Machine Learning Models:** These spot patterns that humans might miss. Example: An algorithm detects subtle changes in vitals that predict sepsis risk before symptoms fully emerge.
- **Natural Language Processing (NLP):** This unlocks insights buried in clinical notes. Example: A CDSS finds a mention of "shortness of breath" in progress notes, factoring it into a differential diagnosis even if it wasn't coded.

Transformative Applications in Healthcare

When used well, CDSS increases precision, improves safety, and aligns care with evolving science.

- **Improving Diagnostic Accuracy:** Systems synthesize symptoms, labs, and history to suggest what might be wrong. Example: A radiology CDSS flags rare diagnoses that match both scan features and recent patient complaints.
- **Enhancing Treatment Effectiveness:** CDSS tailor therapy to patient-specific factors. Example: A drug dosage recommendation adjusts automatically based on kidney function and weight.

- **Reducing Errors and Adverse Events:** Alerts prevent oversights, especially in high-volume settings. Example: A real-time warning stops a doctor from prescribing a medication that conflicts with a known allergy.
- **Facilitating Evidence-Based Medicine:** Systems ingest the latest guidelines so clinicians don't have to memorize them. Example: Treatment plans automatically reflect updated oncology protocols after a major trial is published.

Why This Matters for Trustees

CDSS tools work quietly, but their impact is huge. They reduce malpractice risk, drive better outcomes, and ensure consistency of care, especially across large systems.

But implementation isn't plug-and-play. Trustees need to know whether CDSS tools are clinically validated, well-integrated with workflows, and monitored for accuracy.

When oversight slips, decision support becomes noise. When done right, it becomes invisible, yet invaluable.

Quiz Question

Which of the following is NOT a function typically performed by a Clinical Decision Support System?

- A. Directly performing surgical procedures on patients
- B. Providing alerts for potential drug interactions
- C. Offering diagnostic suggestions based on patient data
- D. Recommending personalized treatment plans

Correct Answer: A
CDSS assists decision-making, it doesn't perform physical procedures like surgery.

Chapter 10

Cloud Computing

The Backbone of Healthcare's Digital Shift

Healthcare used to rely on physical servers, in-house IT teams, and massive data centers. Now, more and more of that is moving to the cloud.

Cloud computing allows healthcare organizations to store, access, and process data using internet-connected servers managed off-site. That means no need to buy and maintain hardware, and far more flexibility when demand spikes.

It's not just about convenience. It's about transforming how hospitals operate, how patients engage, and how data drives decisions.

Core Mechanisms Behind Cloud Computing

Here's what powers cloud systems in healthcare:

- **Data Storage and Management:** Cloud platforms offer elastic, secure storage. Example:

Patient EHRs are stored in the cloud, allowing providers to access them from any facility, instantly.

- **Data Analytics and Processing:** Cloud infrastructure handles computation-heavy tasks quickly and at scale. Example: A public health agency uses cloud analytics to scan thousands of EHRs for emerging disease trends.
- **Collaboration and Telemedicine:** Clinicians can work together in real time, even across continents. Example: A cloud-based telehealth platform connects patients to specialists and shares data instantly across care teams.

Transformative Applications in Healthcare

Cloud computing enables agility, responsiveness, and collaboration across every level of healthcare.

- **Enhanced Data Accessibility and Interoperability:** Everyone sees the same patient data, no matter the location. Example: A traveling patient's provider pulls a complete health record from a cloud-based system without delay.
- **Scalability and Flexibility:** Systems scale up or down based on need, without new hardware. Example: During flu season, cloud servers auto-scale to support increased patient intake and recordkeeping.

- **Innovation and Agility:** Cloud tools launch faster than traditional software. Example: A hospital deploys a COVID-19 vaccine tracking app within days using cloud services.
- **Improved Patient Engagement:** Cloud platforms give patients real-time access to their own data. Example: A mobile app shows patients their lab results and lets them message their physician directly.

Why This Matters for Trustees

Cloud computing is no longer optional, it's foundational.

Hospitals gain speed, savings, and scalability. But they also take on new responsibilities: data governance, vendor oversight, and regulatory compliance. Trustees must ask hard questions about encryption, redundancy, and access control.

Cloud doesn't remove all risks. But it positions healthcare systems to adapt faster, innovate sooner, and deliver care more effectively.

Quiz Question

Which of the following is NOT a benefit of cloud computing in healthcare?

A. Reducing the need for physical storage and on-premises IT infrastructure
B. Completely eliminating cybersecurity risks associated with patient data
C. Enabling real-time data analysis and insights for better decision-making
D. Supporting the deployment and scalability of telemedicine services

Correct Answer: B

The cloud improves security, but it doesn't make risk disappear. Vigilance is still required.

Chapter 11
Data Analytics
Turning Healthcare Data Into Better Decisions

Every day, hospitals generate mountains of data, clinical notes, lab results, imaging scans, billing records, even patient behavior from apps and wearables. On its own, this data is just noise.

But when properly analyzed, it becomes a strategic asset.

Data analytics helps healthcare organizations make sense of the past, anticipate the future, and decide what to do next. It sharpens care, streamlines operations, and helps prevent disease.

Core Mechanisms Behind Data Analytics

There are three main types of analytics driving decisions in healthcare:

- **Descriptive Analytics:** Looks backward to see what happened and why. Example: Hospital leadership reviews trends in ER admissions and length of stay to plan more efficient resource allocation.

- **Predictive Analytics:** Looks ahead, using models to estimate what might happen. Example: A tool flags patients likely to be readmitted within 30 days, prompting early intervention.
- **Prescriptive Analytics:** Suggests what action to take based on predictions. Example: A system recommends a specific treatment based on a patient's lab values, history, and likely outcomes.

Transformative Applications in Healthcare

Data analytics is no longer just for researchers. It's shaping real-time care and policy decisions.

- **Improved Patient Outcomes:** Providers identify risks early and intervene faster. Example: Predictive models catch early signs of diabetes and suggest proactive lifestyle interventions.
- **Enhanced Operational Efficiency:** Leaders use data to run leaner, faster systems. Example: Staffing schedules are adjusted based on historical ER traffic to reduce wait times and staff burnout.

- **Personalized Medicine:** Care is tailored to the patient, not just the condition. Example: Genomic data and clinical history help oncologists select the most effective cancer drug for a specific patient.
- **Public Health and Epidemiology:** Trends guide interventions at scale. Example: Real-time surveillance systems track flu outbreaks and trigger resource shifts before hospitals are overwhelmed.

Why This Matters for Trustees

Healthcare without data analytics is like flying blind. Leaders can't optimize care, cut waste, or spot problems early without the right tools.

Trustees don't need to interpret the data, but they must ensure that analytics systems are accurate, timely, and secure. They should ask how insights are generated, how they're acted on, and who's responsible for results.

Used well, data analytics turns complexity into clarity. And that clarity saves lives.

Quiz Question

Which of the following is NOT an application of data analytics in healthcare?

A. Automatically performing surgeries based on historical success rates
B. Identifying patterns in disease outbreaks to improve public health responses
C. Predicting which patients are at risk of developing certain conditions
D. Optimizing hospital staffing based on patterns of patient admissions

Correct Answer: A

Analytics can guide decisions, but it doesn't perform surgery. That still takes a surgeon's hands.

Chapter 12
Deep Learning
Pushing Healthcare Into the Next Frontier

Deep learning is a subset of AI that mimics how the brain processes information, only at massive scale. It uses neural networks with many layers ("deep" layers) to learn patterns, make predictions, and generate insights from enormous datasets.

In healthcare, this matters because medical data is complex, too complex for traditional software or even human experts to fully interpret. Deep learning systems thrive on that complexity.

They don't just recognize patterns. They find new ones.

Core Mechanisms Behind Deep Learning

Here are the foundational types of deep learning models used in healthcare:

- **Convolutional Neural Networks (CNNs):**
  These are experts in analyzing images.

Example: A CNN scans MRI results to detect tumors faster and more accurately than standard diagnostic tools.

- **Recurrent Neural Networks (RNNs):** These process sequences, perfect for time-based or textual data. Example: An RNN analyzes EHR histories to predict readmission risk after hospital discharge.
- **Generative Adversarial Networks (GANs):** These generate new, realistic data by having two networks compete. Example: GANs create synthetic medical images to train diagnostic models without compromising real patient privacy.

Transformative Applications in Healthcare

Deep learning is no longer experimental. It's already driving change across clinical and operational domains.

- **Enhanced Diagnostic Accuracy:** Models can see things in scans that even trained eyes might miss. Example: A deep learning system flags early signs of diabetic retinopathy from retinal images, prompting earlier interventions.
- **Personalized Treatment Plans:** Models predict individual responses based on past data. Example: A cancer patient's genetic profile is matched with the treatment most likely to produce a positive response.

- **Drug Discovery and Development:** These systems model how molecules behave, before human trials begin. Example: Deep learning helps identify antiviral candidates by simulating how compounds interact with viral proteins.
- **Operational Efficiency:** Beyond the clinic, deep learning improves workflows and planning. Example: Predictive systems forecast which patients are likely to miss appointments, allowing for proactive rescheduling.

Why This Matters for Trustees

Deep learning is more than a buzzword. It's a shift in how healthcare systems understand and act on information.

For trustees, this means oversight. What data trains these models? Are results validated? Who reviews decisions before action is taken? Deep learning offers huge promise, but requires clear governance.

Used well, these systems elevate care. Used blindly, they risk black-box decision-making.

Deep learning doesn't replace clinicians. It gives them sharper tools.

Quiz Question

Which of the following is NOT an application of deep learning in healthcare?

A. Automatically deciding on the best course of treatment without any human oversight
B. Identifying potential drug candidates by predicting molecular interactions
C. Improving the accuracy of diagnosing diseases from medical images
D. Enhancing operational efficiencies by predicting patient no-shows

Correct Answer: A

Deep learning can recommend, but it can't replace clinical judgment or patient choice.

Chapter 13
Digital Health
Bringing Technology to the Center of Care

Digital health isn't a gadget, it's a movement. It's the integration of digital tools and platforms into every layer of healthcare delivery, from prevention to treatment to long-term management.

The goal is simple: make care more personalized, more efficient, and more accessible.

Digital health doesn't replace traditional care. It enhances it, by putting real-time data, remote tools, and patient engagement platforms into everyday use.

Core Mechanisms Behind Digital Health

Digital health is powered by a collection of mature and emerging technologies:

- **Mobile Health (mHealth) Applications:**
  Smartphone apps that support self-care and patient monitoring. Example: An app that

tracks meals and blood glucose levels, offering
personalized feedback for diabetes
management.

- **Wearable Devices:** Tools that collect real-time
  biometric data. Example: A wristband that
  monitors steps, sleep, and heart rate, then syncs
  that data with a patient's medical record.
- **Telehealth and Telemedicine:** Remote
  consultations that break down geographic
  barriers. Example: A psychiatrist conducts
  therapy sessions over video with patients in
  rural communities.
- **Electronic Health Records (EHRs):** Unified,
  accessible patient records across providers.
  Example: A cloud-based EHR system that
  aggregates lab results, prescriptions, and
  imaging from multiple clinics.
- **Big Data and Analytics:** Turning massive
  datasets into actionable insights. Example:
  Public health officials use anonymized data
  from wearables to predict flu season hotspots.

Transformative Applications in Healthcare

Digital health touches nearly every part of the patient
journey, and the provider workflow.

- **Improved Access to Care:** Patients in remote or
  underserved areas get care faster and with
  fewer barriers. Example: A rural patient uses a

telehealth platform to meet with a cardiologist three states away.

- **Enhanced Patient Engagement and Self-Management:** Tools increase adherence and autonomy. Example: An app reminds a patient to take their blood pressure medication and tracks trends over weeks.
- **Data-Driven Healthcare:** Data fuels smarter, more targeted care. Example: Personalized fitness and diet programs are based on a user's wearable device data and health history.
- **Operational Efficiency:** Automation reduces waste and frees up time. Example: AI-powered systems manage appointment scheduling, balancing provider capacity with patient demand.

Why This Matters for Trustees

Digital health isn't a single product, it's a new operating model.

Hospitals that invest wisely in digital health solutions improve care quality, lower operational costs, and boost patient satisfaction. But implementation must be thoughtful. Trustees should ask: Are tools integrated with EHRs? Is patient data secure? Do technologies serve clinical goals?

Done right, digital health doesn't digitize chaos. It simplifies care.

Quiz Question

Which of the following is NOT an objective of digital health?

    A. To replace traditional healthcare services entirely with digital solutions
    B. To improve access to healthcare services, especially for underserved populations
    C. To enhance patient engagement and empower individuals to manage their health
    D. To leverage data and analytics for better healthcare decision-making and personalized medicine

Correct Answer: A

Digital health complements, not replaces, traditional care. It integrates digital tools to support better outcomes.

Chapter 14

Digital Twins

**Simulating Healthcare for Smarter,
Safer Decisions**

A digital twin is a virtual replica of a physical object, process, or system that mirrors its real-world counterpart in real time. In healthcare, digital twins can represent anything from a patient's physiology to a hospital's operating room workflow.

By simulating different scenarios within a digital twin, whether for care delivery or infrastructure optimization, healthcare organizations can test outcomes, reduce risk, and make data-driven decisions before taking action in the real world.

Core Mechanisms Behind Digital Twins

Digital twins rely on several foundational technologies to function effectively:

- **Real-Time Data Integration:** Sensors, wearables, EHRs, and IoT devices feed

continuous data into the digital model.
Example: A digital twin of a cardiac patient
receives real-time updates from their wearable
heart monitor and medication regimen.

- **Simulation and Modeling Engines:** Advanced
  physics or AI models simulate real-world
  behavior based on inputs. Example: A clinician
  can simulate different drug therapies for a
  cancer patient to assess likely tumor response
  before choosing a treatment.
- **Feedback Loops and Machine Learning:** The
  system learns and refines its predictions based
  on real-world outcomes. Example: A hospital's
  surgical suite twin adapts to show better
  workflows after several weeks of observation
  and algorithmic learning.

Transformative Applications in Healthcare

Digital twins can be deployed across clinical, operational,
and research domains.

- **Personalized Patient Care:** Twins model how a
  specific individual's body might respond to
  treatments. Example: A neurologist uses a brain
  digital twin to plan epilepsy surgery, modeling
  seizure pathways and electrode placements in
  advance.
- **Hospital Operations and Capacity Planning:**
  Twins help simulate hospital throughput,

staffing, and resource allocation. Example: A hospital runs simulations in its digital twin to prepare for a flu surge, testing supply levels, staff shifts, and bed usage in advance.

- **Medical Device Development:** Simulated patients accelerate testing without risking real lives. Example: A medical device company tests pacemaker behavior across digital models of patients with varying arrhythmia types.
- **Training and Clinical Decision Support:** Trainees and clinicians can experiment in a zero-risk virtual environment. Example: A digital twin of a high-risk pregnancy allows obstetricians to train on complications using real-time vitals and fetal responses.

Why This Matters for Trustees

Digital twins align with every board-level concern: safety, efficiency, patient outcomes, and financial performance. They allow hospitals to test assumptions before implementing policies, prepare for high-impact events, and customize care at scale.

Trustees should ask: Are we collecting the kind of real-time data needed to support digital twin development? Are we working with vendors or institutions to develop simulations that match our patient population or facility layout?

A digital twin won't replace clinical experience. But it will sharpen every decision your team makes, from the bedside to the boardroom.

Quiz Question

Which of the following is NOT a typical use of a digital twin in healthcare?

- A. Simulating patient responses to different treatment options
- B. Optimizing surgical workflow and room usage based on predictive modeling
- C. Automatically performing surgeries without clinician involvement
- D. Training healthcare professionals using real-time virtual models

Correct Answer: C

Digital twins support simulation and prediction, but they don't perform physical procedures. Surgery still requires skilled human professionals.

Chapter 15
Edge Computing
Bringing Real-Time Intelligence to the Patient's Side

Edge computing in healthcare refers to the processing of data closer to the source, such as bedside monitors, wearables, or imaging devices, rather than sending all information to a centralized server or cloud for analysis. This allows decisions to be made faster, with lower latency and reduced dependency on constant connectivity.

In a hospital, edge computing can mean the difference between seconds and minutes when detecting a critical event. It's a key enabler of real-time monitoring, smart diagnostics, and decentralized care.

Core Mechanisms Behind Edge Computing

Edge computing relies on three technical components working in tandem:

- **Local Processing Nodes:** Small computers or chips embedded in medical devices or local servers. Example: A portable ultrasound machine equipped with edge processing can analyze images instantly, even in the field.

- **Low-Latency Architecture:** Reduces data transmission time by avoiding the cloud roundtrip. Example: A bedside monitor detects respiratory distress and alerts staff within milliseconds, without needing to "check in" with a cloud-based AI.
- **Selective Cloud Syncing:** Only critical or filtered data is sent to the cloud for long-term storage or broader analysis. Example: A hospital bed's pressure sensor logs all activity locally but only uploads risk flags to the EHR system.

Transformative Applications in Healthcare

Edge computing powers both clinical and operational improvements.

- **Faster Response in Critical Care:** Decisions can be made on-site with minimal delay. Example: A cardiac monitoring system at the patient's bedside processes ECG data in real time, sounding an alert before a nurse or provider even reaches the screen.
- **Improved Data Resilience and Privacy:** Less dependency on external networks means fewer risks. Example: An ambulance uses edge

devices to process trauma data en route to the hospital, without needing continuous internet.

- **Enhanced Imaging and Diagnostics:** Speeds up interpretation and reduces backlogs. Example: A mobile radiology unit instantly processes scans and flags abnormalities for a radiologist review before the patient leaves.
- **Remote and Rural Care Support:** Enables care in areas with poor connectivity. Example: A rural clinic with intermittent internet still uses AI-assisted diagnostic tools locally via edge computing nodes.

Why This Matters for Trustees

Edge computing is not a buzzword, it's an infrastructure layer critical to speed, safety, and reliability. It supports care continuity during outages, accelerates diagnostics, and reduces the load on centralized IT systems.

Trustees should ask: Are we over-relying on the cloud for real-time care? Are our devices edge-capable? Is our IT infrastructure aligned with our clinical urgency needs?

Edge computing doesn't replace cloud computing. It complements it, bringing rapid intelligence to the point of care.

Quiz Question

Which of the following is NOT a benefit of edge computing in healthcare?

- A. Processing patient data locally to enable real-time alerts
- B. Reducing latency in critical care decision-making
- C. Eliminating the need for data backup or cloud connectivity
- D. Supporting diagnostics in low-connectivity or rural environments

Correct Answer: C

Edge computing reduces dependence on the cloud for real-time use, but data still needs to be backed up and integrated centrally for continuity and long-term access.

Chapter 16
Electronic Health Records
The Digital Core of Modern Healthcare

Electronic Health Records (EHRs) have replaced paper charts as the foundation of patient information in modern medicine. They're real-time, digital, and accessible across care teams, making them essential to how healthcare is delivered today.

At their best, EHRs make care more informed, more coordinated, and safer.

They don't just store data. They connect it, across clinicians, systems, and even patients themselves.

Core Mechanisms Behind EHRs

Here's what makes EHRs function beyond a digital filing cabinet:

- **Digital Documentation:** Patient information is digitized and centralized. Example: A full record of allergies, lab results, prescriptions, and imaging is stored in one secure system.

- **Interoperability:** Data can move between providers and facilities in real time. Example: A primary care physician shares a patient's chart with a specialist across town before a consultation.
- **Patient Portals:** Patients can see and manage their own health data. Example: A user logs in to view lab results, refill prescriptions, and send messages to their care team.

Transformative Applications in Healthcare

EHRs have done more than digitize paperwork, they've reshaped care delivery.

- **Improved Patient Care:** With full history in hand, clinicians make faster, safer decisions. Example: A doctor sees a patient's drug allergy history immediately before prescribing antibiotics.
- **Enhanced Efficiency:** Fewer forms, fewer faxes, fewer duplicate tests. Example: A radiologist uploads imaging directly into the EHR, cutting turnaround time by days.
- **Data Analytics and Research:** Large-scale trends become visible across systems. Example: Researchers use anonymized EHR data to

assess which treatments are most effective in real-world settings.

- **Increased Patient Participation:** Patients manage their own care more actively. Example: Through a portal, a patient tracks blood pressure readings and sends updates to their cardiologist.

Why This Matters for Trustees

EHRs are the infrastructure that ties modern care together. They influence quality, safety, cost, and even patient satisfaction.

Trustees should ensure that systems are interoperable, secure, and actually used by clinicians, not just installed for compliance. They must also support patient-facing features like portals that drive engagement and transparency.

EHRs are not a one-time investment. They're a platform that needs constant refinement.

Quiz Question

Which of the following statements about EHRs is flase?

- A. EHRs allow for real-time sharing of patient information across healthcare providers
- B. EHRs eliminate the need for patients to be involved in their healthcare management
- C. EHRs contribute to research by providing a rich source of aggregated data for analysis
- D. EHRs enhance patient care by providing comprehensive health information

Correct Answer: B

EHRs don't sideline patients, they help bring them into the process through access and engagement.

Chapter 17
Generative AI
Creating the Future of Healthcare

Generative AI doesn't just analyze data, it creates new content from it. That includes text, images, sounds, and even synthetic data. In healthcare, this ability unlocks new frontiers in research, diagnostics, training, and personalized care.

It's not about replacing clinicians. It's about giving them tools to simulate, model, and test more, before making real-world decisions.

Generative AI brings speed, scale, and creativity to problems that used to take years to solve.

Core Mechanisms Behind Generative AI

Here are the main models powering this shift:

- **Generative Adversarial Networks (GANs):** Two neural networks, one generates, one critiques, until the output looks real. Example: GANs create synthetic X-rays for training algorithms, without using actual patient data.

- **Variational Autoencoders (VAEs):** These compress and recreate data, learning its patterns to produce new variants. Example: VAEs generate novel genetic sequences for studying how gene mutations affect disease.
- **Transformer Models:** These excel at understanding and generating human language. Example: A transformer generates patient-doctor dialogue for training empathy in medical professionals.

Transformative Applications in Healthcare

Generative AI is already reshaping how medicine is developed, delivered, and learned.

- **Synthetic Data Generation:** Safe, realistic data without privacy concerns. Example: A health system trains an AI tool on synthetic EHRs, ensuring no real patient data is exposed.
- **Drug Discovery and Development:** AI proposes entirely new molecules to test in silico. Example: A model explores chemical structures to find compounds that could neutralize a new virus strain.
- **Personalized Medicine:** Patient-specific simulations predict how treatments might perform. Example: A virtual patient model

helps oncologists compare likely outcomes of multiple treatment plans.

- **Medical Imaging and Diagnostics:** Enhances what clinicians see and how early they see it. Example: Low-resolution MRI scans are refined with AI to spot small tumors that might otherwise be missed.

Why This Matters for Trustees

Generative AI is a leap, not a step, in healthcare innovation. But it needs clear boundaries.

Trustees must ensure clinical oversight stays intact, especially when synthetic content informs real decisions. They should ask: Is the model explainable? Is the output validated? How is bias mitigated?

Generative AI is a multiplier, but without good guardrails, it can scale bad assumptions just as easily as good ones.

Used wisely, it doesn't just speed up medicine. It improves it.

Quiz Question

Which of the following is NOT an application of generative AI in healthcare?

A. Generating synthetic patient data for privacy-sensitive research
B. Directly providing medical advice to patients without human oversight
C. Creating high-resolution medical images from lower-quality scans
D. Accelerating the discovery of new drugs through molecular structure prediction

Correct Answer: B

Generative AI supports care, but doesn't replace licensed professionals making final medical decisions.

Chapter 18

Health Information Exchange

Connecting the Dots Across Healthcare

Health Information Exchange (HIE) is how patient data moves securely across different healthcare systems. It lets hospitals, clinics, pharmacies, and patients share information in real time, regardless of the software they use.

This isn't just a tech upgrade. HIE enables safer, faster, and more coordinated care.

When systems can talk to each other, patients don't fall through the cracks.

Core Mechanisms Behind HIE

There are three main ways HIE makes data accessible across healthcare settings:

- **Direct Exchange:** One provider sends data securely to another. Example: A primary care doctor emails a patient's full medical history to a specialist ahead of a referral visit.

- **Query-Based Exchange:** A provider searches for and retrieves a patient's records when needed. Example: An ER physician pulls medication history from another hospital during an emergency.
- **Consumer-Mediated Exchange:** Patients control and share their own data. Example: A patient uses a health app to send lab results from one clinic to another for a second opinion.

Transformative Applications in Healthcare

HIE isn't about data, it's about decisions. The right data at the right time improves care.

- **Improved Care Coordination:** Providers operate from a single, shared view of the patient. Example: A hospital discharge summary goes directly to the patient's outpatient care team to guide follow-up.
- **Enhanced Patient Safety:** Complete information prevents dangerous oversights. Example: An alert flags a life-threatening allergy before medication is administered in the ER.
- **Reduced Redundant Testing:** Providers see what's already been done. Example: A specialist skips ordering another MRI by accessing one completed last month.

- **Support for Public Health and Research:**
  Aggregate data supports large-scale health insights. Example: Real-time flu data from multiple hospitals helps monitor regional outbreaks and vaccine performance.

Why This Matters for Trustees

HIE solves one of healthcare's oldest problems: fragmentation. When systems don't talk, care breaks down.

Trustees should prioritize HIE integration across their networks. Ask: Are all care settings connected? Is patient consent handled clearly? How is data quality and security maintained?

Without HIE, patients carry their medical history by memory. With HIE, it's always where it needs to be.

Quiz Question

Which of the following is NOT a direct benefit of Health Information Exchange?

- A. Eliminating the need for patients to visit healthcare providers in person
- B. Improving care coordination among different healthcare professionals
- C. Reducing unnecessary tests and procedures by sharing patient information
- D. Enhancing patient safety by providing comprehensive medical histories at the point of care

Correct Answer: A

HIE improves how data moves, but it doesn't replace in-person care when physical exams or treatments are required.

Chapter 19
Health Informatics
The Engine Behind Smarter, Safer Healthcare

Health informatics is where healthcare meets technology and data. It's the science of how information is collected, shared, and used to improve care, cut costs, and make systems run better.

It's not just about digital tools. It's about redesigning the way healthcare works, through smarter systems and informed decision-making.

Informatics supports everything from clinical care to research to policy. And when it's done right, everyone benefits.

Core Mechanisms Behind Health Informatics

These are the core technologies that drive informatics in real-world healthcare settings:

- **Electronic Health Records (EHRs):** Digital patient charts that follow the patient across providers. Example: A hospital system pulls together lab results, imaging, and prescriptions from multiple facilities into a single, comprehensive patient record.

- **Clinical Decision Support Systems (CDSS):** Real-time alerts and recommendations powered by patient data. Example: A CDSS flags a drug interaction risk before a prescription is finalized, preventing an adverse reaction.
- **Health Information Exchange (HIE):** Seamless sharing of data across institutions. Example: A walk-in clinic accesses a patient's immunization record from another health network in seconds.

Transformative Applications in Healthcare

Health informatics isn't just back-end IT, it directly impacts care quality, speed, and patient experience.

- **Improved Patient Safety and Quality of Care:** Fewer errors, better diagnostics, safer treatments. Example: An EHR system cross-checks for allergies and prior medications before a new drug is prescribed.
- **Enhanced Healthcare Efficiency:** Less paperwork, faster workflows, fewer repeat procedures. Example: An automated scheduling tool reduces patient no-shows by sending real-time appointment reminders.

- **Data-Driven Insights and Innovations:** Big data becomes clinical insight. Example: Analytics teams study chronic disease trends to inform population health initiatives.
- **Empowered Patients and Personalized Care:** Informed patients make better decisions. Example: A patient uses a portal to check test results, message their doctor, and manage follow-up care independently.

Why This Matters for Trustees

Health informatics is the infrastructure behind modern care delivery. It touches every function, clinical, operational, strategic.

Trustees must ensure these systems are interoperable, secure, and patient-centered. They should ask: How well do our systems talk to each other? Are we using data to improve care, or just storing it?

Informatics doesn't replace providers. It equips them to do their jobs better, faster, and more safely.

Quiz Question

Which of the following is NOT a goal of health informatics?

A. Eliminating the need for healthcare professionals by fully automating patient care
B. Enhancing the quality and safety of patient care through better data management
C. Improving healthcare efficiency by optimizing workflows and reducing unnecessary tests
D. Empowering patients with access to their health information for informed decision-making

Correct Answer: A

Health informatics supports, not replaces, clinicians. It strengthens care by improving the flow and use of information.

Chapter 20
Hospital at Home
**Bringing Acute Care to the
Living Room**

The Hospital at Home (HaH) model delivers hospital-level care in the patient's own home. What started as a solution for older adults has expanded into a flexible model that works across conditions, ages, and communities.

It's not just home care. It's hospital care, without the building.

HaH reduces costs, increases comfort, and improves outcomes by blending technology, in-person visits, and coordinated care.

Core Mechanisms Behind Hospital at Home

The model works by integrating four core components:

- **Remote Monitoring Technologies:** Real-time data from the home to the care team. Example: A wearable device tracks blood pressure and oxygen levels, sending updates to clinicians every hour.

- **Telehealth and Virtual Visits:** Daily touchpoints without the drive or wait room. Example: A physician checks in each morning via video, reviews the patient's condition, and adjusts medications.
- **Mobile Health Teams:** On-the-ground care for procedures and assessments. Example: A nurse visits to administer IV antibiotics and change wound dressings.
- **Integrated Care Coordination:** One system to manage it all, visits, monitoring, logistics. Example: A coordinator schedules home visits, ensures equipment is delivered, and keeps the care team aligned.

Transformative Applications in Healthcare

Hospital at Home is reshaping how we think about hospitalization, and who actually needs to be in a hospital bed.

- **Reduced Hospital Readmissions and Complications:** Home care can prevent the risks that come with inpatient stays. Example: Heart failure patients managed at home avoid infection risks and receive more tailored education.
- **Enhanced Patient Satisfaction and Comfort:** Patients prefer their beds to hospital beds.

Example: A terminally ill patient receives palliative care at home, surrounded by loved ones in a familiar setting.

- **Cost-Effectiveness:** Less overhead, fewer unnecessary labs, and shorter durations of care. Example: Treating mild pneumonia at home saves thousands in hospitalization costs without sacrificing outcomes.
- **Increased Access to Care:** HaH reaches patients in care deserts. Example: A rural patient receives hospital-grade monitoring and interventions without traveling miles to the nearest facility.

Why This Matters for Trustees

Hospital at Home is not fringe, it's the future of acute care delivery.

It aligns with strategic goals: reduce cost, increase patient satisfaction, and improve outcomes. But success depends on infrastructure, staffing, and regulatory clarity. Trustees should ask: Are reimbursement models aligned? Are remote monitoring systems reliable? Are care teams equipped for in-home complexity?

Done well, HaH shifts the center of gravity in healthcare, from the facility to the patient.

Quiz Question

Which of the following is NOT a typical benefit of the Hospital at Home model?

A. Providing patients with the same level of social activities as they would experience in a hospital setting

B. Reducing the risk of hospital-acquired infections by treating patients in their own homes

C. Enhancing patient satisfaction by offering personalized care in a comfortable environment

D. Potentially lowering healthcare costs compared to traditional hospital stays

Correct Answer: A

HaH delivers medical care, not hospital social programs. Its value lies in outcomes, comfort, and efficiency.

Chapter 21
The Internet of Things
Building a Connected Healthcare Ecosystem

The Internet of Things (IoT) in healthcare links devices, software, and systems through the internet to enable real-time data sharing and monitoring. It connects patients to providers, devices to dashboards, and data to decisions.

IoT isn't about gadgets. It's about smarter, faster, more responsive care.

From remote monitoring to inventory tracking, IoT is turning healthcare into a real-time service.

Core Mechanisms Behind IoT

These are the foundational components that make IoT work in healthcare:

- **Sensors and Wearable Devices:** Track vital signs and activity continuously. Example: A continuous glucose monitor alerts patients and providers when blood sugar falls outside the safe range.

- **Remote Monitoring Systems:** Deliver virtual oversight from a distance. Example: A cardiologist receives alerts if a heart failure patient's pulse patterns show signs of decompensation.
- **Connected Medical Devices:** Devices communicate and log usage data automatically. Example: A smart inhaler tracks when and how often it's used, helping physicians monitor asthma control.

Transformative Applications in Healthcare

IoT touches nearly every part of the patient experience and provider workflow.

- **Improved Patient Monitoring and Care:** Conditions are managed in real time, not just at checkups. Example: A home RPM system sends alerts to care teams when heart rate, weight, or blood pressure suddenly change.
- **Enhanced Patient Engagement and Compliance:** Devices guide behavior and track adherence. Example: A smart pill dispenser reminds patients to take medication and logs whether they did.
- **Operational Efficiency and Cost Reduction:** Facilities run smoother with less waste.

Example: IoT-enabled inventory sensors automatically reorder medical supplies before stock runs out.

- **Data-Driven Insights for Personalized Care:** Behavioral data informs tailored interventions. Example: Activity and sleep data from a wearable help personalize recovery plans for orthopedic patients.

Why This Matters for Trustees

IoT is a force multiplier, it amplifies clinical capacity, improves continuity of care, and cuts unnecessary costs. But with this power comes complexity.

Trustees must ensure device interoperability, secure data handling, and patient consent policies are in place. Ask: Are we collecting meaningful data? Is it being acted on? Who owns the device-generated data?

IoT doesn't replace doctors. It equips them to intervene earlier, act faster, and care better.

Quiz Question

Which of the following is NOT a direct benefit of integrating IoT in healthcare?

A. Reducing the need for in-person doctor visits through remote monitoring
B. Completely replacing the role of healthcare professionals with automated systems
C. Enhancing patient engagement and medication adherence through smart devices
D. Improving the management and allocation of healthcare resources

Correct Answer: B

IoT enhances care, but it doesn't replace the need for trained human oversight in diagnosis and treatment.

Chapter 22
Interoperability
Making Healthcare Systems Speak the Same Language

Interoperability in healthcare is the foundation that allows different information systems, software applications, and networks to communicate and work together. It's not just about sharing data, it's about understanding it, using it, and making better decisions because of it.

At its core, interoperability is what allows a patient's health information to follow them, no matter where they go. It bridges the gap between fragmented systems, enabling continuity of care, better outcomes, and more efficient operations.

Core Mechanisms Behind Interoperability

True interoperability depends on alignment across technical standards, shared meaning, and governance structures.

- **Syntactic Interoperability:** This is about structure, getting systems to exchange data in the same format. Example: Two EHR platforms using HL7 or FHIR standards can send lab results, prescriptions, and clinical notes to one another without reformatting.
- **Semantic Interoperability:** This is about meaning, ensuring the receiving system understands the data the same way. Example: One system records "MI" and another says "heart attack," but both are recognized as "Myocardial Infarction" using SNOMED CT mappings.
- **Organizational Interoperability:** This is about policies and governance, ensuring secure, lawful, and seamless data sharing. Example: A regional health system creates agreements that let hospitals, outpatient clinics, and labs exchange data while complying with HIPAA.

These three layers work together to allow accurate, effective, and meaningful data exchange across the healthcare ecosystem.

Transformative Applications in Healthcare

Interoperability isn't just a technical achievement. It enables real-world benefits for patients, providers, and public health.

- **Enhanced Patient Care:** Providers get a complete picture of the patient's medical history. Example: A primary care doctor pulls recent hospital discharge notes to adjust medications and schedule appropriate follow-ups.
- **Improved Public Health Monitoring and Response:** Data moves faster than disease when systems are interoperable. Example: Health departments receive real-time updates on flu and COVID-19 trends, enabling targeted responses and resource allocation.
- **Increased Healthcare Efficiency and Reduced Costs:** Redundant tests and procedures are avoided. Example: A radiologist accesses prior MRIs from a referring hospital rather than ordering another scan, saving money and patient time.
- **Patient Empowerment and Engagement:** Interoperability supports health literacy and engagement by making data accessible. Example: A patient uses a portal to share lab results from a private provider with their primary care team before a consultation.

Why This Matters for Trustees

Interoperability isn't optional, it's strategic infrastructure. It affects everything from clinical outcomes to regulatory compliance to cost containment.

Trustees should ask: Are our systems interoperable within the network and outside it? Are we using national standards like FHIR? Are data governance policies in place to ensure security without stifling information flow?

Without interoperability, each provider works from an incomplete story. With it, care becomes connected, efficient, and data-driven.

Quiz Question

Which of the following is NOT a benefit of healthcare interoperability?

A. Increased duplication of medical tests
B. Enhanced patient care through comprehensive health records
C. Improved public health monitoring and response
D. Reduced healthcare delivery costs

Correct Answer: A

Interoperability is designed to eliminate redundant testing, not increase it, by giving providers access to a patient's full medical history.

Chapter 23
Machine Learning
The Intelligence Layer Behind Healthcare Innovation

Machine Learning (ML) is a form of artificial intelligence that enables computers to learn from data, recognize patterns, and make decisions without being explicitly programmed for each task. In healthcare, it powers everything from predictive analytics to personalized treatments.

The strength of ML is its ability to adapt, learning more as more data becomes available.

It doesn't just automate tasks. It continuously improves them.

Core Mechanisms Behind Machine Learning

ML includes three major learning types, each serving different healthcare roles:

- **Supervised Learning:** Algorithms train on labeled datasets to predict outcomes. Example: A model learns to detect malignant tumors by training on thousands of labeled radiology images.

- **Unsupervised Learning:** Algorithms find patterns without predefined labels. Example: Clustering patients based on shared characteristics to uncover new disease subtypes.
- **Reinforcement Learning:** Models learn through trial and error in simulated environments. Example: An AI system simulates different chronic care strategies, adjusting based on patient response outcomes.

Transformative Applications in Healthcare

Machine learning is at the core of many next-generation tools in clinical care and operations.

- **Predictive Analytics for Patient Management:** Forecasting future health risks. Example: An ML algorithm identifies patients at high risk for developing diabetes in the next five years.
- **Enhanced Diagnostic Accuracy:** ML improves image interpretation beyond human limits. Example: A deep learning model detects early pneumonia on chest X-rays before radiologists flag it.
- **Personalized Medicine:** Treatment is tailored to the individual, not the average. Example: Predicting chemotherapy response based on a patient's genetic data and medical history.

- **Operational Efficiency in Healthcare Facilities:** Smarter scheduling and workflow automation. Example: ML software optimizes appointment calendars, maximizing throughput and minimizing idle time.

Why This Matters for Trustees

ML is embedded in diagnostics, scheduling, risk scoring, and patient engagement. Trustees must ensure transparency and governance around its use.

Ask: How is the model trained? What biases may exist in the data? Who reviews model decisions before action is taken?

ML is not just about speed, it's about better decisions, made earlier and more accurately.

Quiz Question

Which of the following best describes an application of unsupervised learning in healthcare?

- A. Predicting patient treatment outcomes using labeled datasets
- B. Detecting fraudulent claims in insurance billing with no prior labeling
- C. Customizing drug prescriptions based on genetic information
- D. Scheduling patient appointments to maximize hospital resource use

Correct Answer: B

Unsupervised learning detects hidden patterns in unlabeled data, ideal for spotting fraud or anomalies.

Chapter 24
Mobile Health (mHealth)
Healthcare in Your Pocket

Mobile health, or mHealth, is the use of mobile devices, like smartphones, tablets, and wearables, to deliver and support healthcare. It includes everything from telemedicine apps to fitness trackers, helping patients access care, monitor their health, and stay connected to providers.

What makes mHealth powerful is its reach. It breaks down barriers of location, cost, and complexity, bringing care to people wherever they are.

It's not a replacement for healthcare. It's a layer that makes it faster, smarter, and more patient-driven.

Core Mechanisms Behind mHealth

Several core technologies define how mHealth functions today:

- **Telehealth and Telemedicine Apps:** Allow patients to consult providers without leaving home. Example: A patient uses a video consultation app for follow-up care, avoiding a trip to the clinic.

- **Health Monitoring and Wellness Apps:** Track metrics like heart rate, sleep, and steps. Example: A fitness app monitors daily activity and encourages users to meet custom health goals.
- **Medication Management Apps:** Support adherence with reminders and tracking features. Example: An app sends push notifications when it's time for a patient to take their blood pressure medication.
- **Access to Health Information:** Gives patients real-time access to their medical records and educational content. Example: A patient logs into a mobile portal to view lab results and send a secure message to their provider.

Transformative Applications in Healthcare

mHealth is changing how healthcare is accessed, delivered, and experienced.

- **Improved Access to Care:** mHealth connects patients to care in places traditional medicine doesn't reach. Example: Rural patients use a mobile app to speak with a doctor and get prescriptions filled remotely.

- **Enhanced Patient Engagement and Empowerment:** Patients take a more active role in their care. Example: A diabetes management app tracks blood sugar, logs meals, and educates users about glycemic control.
- **Increased Healthcare Efficiency:** Reduces paperwork, no-shows, and scheduling friction. Example: An mHealth system sends automated appointment reminders and allows patients to reschedule via text.
- **Real-time Health Monitoring and Intervention:** Preventive care becomes proactive, not reactive. Example: A wearable detects abnormal heart rhythms and alerts the user to contact a physician immediately.

Why This Matters for Trustees

mHealth is where healthcare meets daily life. Its growth is inevitable, and it's already influencing patient expectations and care models.

Trustees should ask: Are our systems optimized for mobile access? Are we vetting apps for security, privacy, and clinical value? Are we using mHealth data to personalize care?

Mobile platforms give patients power. Used wisely, they also give providers reach, insight, and efficiency.

Quiz Question

Which of the following is NOT a typical use of mobile health (mHealth)?

- A. Conducting surgical procedures remotely via a smartphone app
- B. Providing medication management and adherence reminders
- C. Facilitating virtual consultations with healthcare providers
- D. Tracking physical activity and dietary intake

Correct Answer: A

mHealth supports care, it doesn't replace complex, in-person procedures like surgery.

Chapter 25
Nanotechnology
Precision Medicine at the Molecular Scale

Nanotechnology in healthcare, often called nanomedicine, operates at the scale of atoms and molecules to transform how we diagnose, treat, and even prevent disease. It allows clinicians and researchers to work at the cellular level with unprecedented precision.

This isn't about shrinking existing tools. It's about redesigning interventions from the ground up using nanoscale materials that behave differently than their larger counterparts.

By targeting disease at its source, nanotechnology holds the potential to increase effectiveness, reduce side effects, and open doors to therapies once considered impossible.

Core Mechanisms Behind Nanotechnology

Nanotechnology is not one tool, it's a platform that spans drug delivery, diagnostics, and tissue regeneration.

- **Nanoparticles for Drug Delivery:** Deliver medication directly to the problem site. Example: Liposomal nanoparticles carry chemotherapy drugs straight to tumor cells, reducing harm to healthy tissue.
- **Nanomaterials for Imaging and Diagnostics:** Boost the accuracy of scans and tests. Example: Quantum dots help surgeons precisely map tumor boundaries during cancer surgery.
- **Nanofibers for Tissue Engineering:** Provide a framework for tissue repair and regeneration. Example: Electrospun nanofibers mimic the body's natural structures to accelerate skin healing.
- **Nanosensors for Health Monitoring:** Detect changes at the molecular level in real time. Example: A glucose-monitoring nanosensor embedded in a contact lens alerts diabetic patients of high blood sugar.

Transformative Applications in Healthcare

Nanotechnology is not hypothetical. It's already reshaping how we approach diagnosis, therapy, and recovery.

- **Targeted Cancer Therapies:** Treatment goes directly to cancer cells, no more carpet bombing. Example: Gold nanoparticles deliver RNA therapy to silence genes that fuel tumor growth.

- **Advanced Diagnostic Tools:** Detect disease early, sometimes before symptoms start. Example: Nanoparticle-based tests identify Alzheimer's-related proteins in blood samples years before cognitive decline.
- **Regenerative Medicine:** Restore what was lost or damaged with nanoscale building blocks. Example: Nanoscaffolds help regenerate nerve tissue in spinal cord injuries by guiding cellular repair.
- **Personalized Medicine:** Tailor treatment to a patient's unique molecular profile. Example: Nanoparticles designed to deliver cancer drugs that match specific genetic mutations in an individual's tumor.

Why This Matters for Trustees

Nanomedicine is not just about cutting-edge science. It's about increasing precision, lowering toxicity, and improving patient outcomes across the board.

Trustees should monitor how nanotechnology is being incorporated into research, diagnostics, and therapeutics at their institutions. Key questions include: Are there partnerships with academic nanotech labs? Are clinicians equipped to understand and adopt nanotech-based tools? Are regulatory and ethical frameworks in place?

The challenge is scale. The opportunity is transformation.

Quiz Question

Which of the following is NOT a current application of nanotechnology in healthcare?

- A. Enhancing physical strength and endurance through nanobot-enhanced muscle fibers
- B. Delivering drugs directly to cancer cells using nanoparticles
- C. Using nanomaterials to improve the sensitivity of diagnostic imaging
- D. Creating scaffolds for tissue regeneration with nanofibers

Correct Answer: A

While nanotechnology is advancing rapidly, human performance enhancement via nanobot muscle augmentation is not a current clinical application.

Chapter 26
Natural Language Processing
Unlocking Healthcare's Unstructured Data

Natural Language Processing (NLP) is a branch of artificial intelligence that enables machines to understand, interpret, and generate human language. In healthcare, where vast amounts of critical data are buried in free-text notes, reports, and patient feedback, NLP offers a way to extract meaning and turn words into action.

More than 80% of healthcare data is unstructured. That includes clinical notes, discharge summaries, referral letters, and research articles. NLP makes that data searchable, analyzable, and useful.

It's how language becomes insight, and insight becomes care.

Core Mechanisms Behind NLP

NLP tools function through several core capabilities:

- **Text Analysis and Classification:**
  Automatically processes and organizes large
  volumes of free text. Example: Patient
  comments are classified as compliments,
  complaints, or suggestions, helping
  organizations target service improvements.
- **Entity Recognition:** Identifies key medical
  terms, drug names, and conditions in text.
  Example: Extracting "Metformin 500mg twice
  daily" from a physician's note and linking it to
  the patient's active medication list.
- **Sentiment Analysis:** Gauges emotions or
  attitudes expressed in text data. Example:
  Monitoring online patient reviews to assess
  sentiment trends around care quality at
  different facilities.

These mechanisms allow unstructured data to be
indexed, categorized, and linked to structured systems like
electronic health records (EHRs).

Transformative Applications in Healthcare

NLP is already helping clinicians, administrators, and
public health officials do more with less.

- **Enhanced Clinical Documentation:** Speeds up
  and improves the accuracy of medical records.
  Example: A doctor dictates a note during a visit;

NLP converts it into a structured EHR entry with medications, diagnoses, and follow-up plans.

- **Improved Patient Care:** Supports clinical decisions with relevant information at the point of care. Example: NLP tools summarize years of clinical notes into a short digest before a provider sees a complex patient.
- **Data-Driven Insights for Public Health:** Turns social chatter and clinician reports into trend signals. Example: Public health officials analyze Reddit and Twitter posts for keywords related to flu symptoms to detect regional outbreaks earlier.
- **Personalized Patient Communication:** Adjusts tone, vocabulary, and content to meet patient needs. Example: A post-surgery care summary is automatically rewritten to match a sixth-grade reading level for improved understanding.

Why This Matters for Trustees

NLP expands what can be done with the data you already have. It transforms clinical text into structured, usable insights, improving outcomes and reducing administrative waste.

Trustees should ensure their organizations are equipped to implement NLP tools responsibly. Are data pipelines secure? Is the output validated by clinicians? Is bias monitored in text interpretation?

NLP doesn't generate new data. It unlocks the value hidden in the words already written.

Quiz Question

Which of the following is NOT a typical application of NLP in healthcare?

- A. Translating patient records into multiple languages automatically
- B. Predicting disease outbreaks by analyzing weather data
- C. Summarizing patient medical histories for quick reference by healthcare providers
- D. Analyzing patient feedback to identify areas for service improvement

Correct Answer: B

Weather data analysis relies on traditional data science, not natural language processing, which focuses on textual content.

Chapter 27
Pharmacogenetics
Personalizing Medication Through Genetic Insight

Pharmacogenetics is the science of how an individual's genetic makeup influences their response to medications. Rather than relying on trial and error, this field aims to predict which drugs will work best, and which might cause harm, based on your DNA.

It's not futuristic. It's happening now. And it's changing how medications are prescribed.

By understanding genetic variations that affect drug metabolism, response, and sensitivity, pharmacogenetics is creating a new standard: one patient, one genome, one optimized treatment plan.

Core Mechanisms Behind Pharmacogenetics

Here are the core ways pharmacogenetics guides clinical decisions:

- **Genetic Variability in Drug Metabolism:** Some patients metabolize drugs too quickly, others too slowly. Example: Testing for CYP2C19 variants helps determine if a patient can effectively metabolize clopidogrel, a common blood thinner.
- **Genetic Markers for Drug Efficacy:** Certain gene profiles predict whether a medication will be effective. Example: Identifying patients with specific EGFR mutations to determine eligibility for targeted lung cancer therapies.
- **Genetic Testing for Drug Sensitivity:** Screens for variants that can trigger dangerous side effects. Example: Patients with the HLA-B*5701 allele are at risk for severe allergic reactions to the HIV drug abacavir, and should avoid it.

Transformative Applications in Healthcare

Pharmacogenetics is turning "personalized medicine" from buzzword into practice.

- **Personalized Drug Therapy:** Medications and doses are adjusted to your genetic code. Example: Warfarin, a blood thinner, is notoriously tricky to dose. Genetic testing helps customize it to reduce the risk of stroke or bleeding.
- **Improved Medication Safety:** Reduces hospitalizations and adverse events caused by

incompatible prescriptions. Example: Screening before prescribing carbamazepine prevents life-threatening skin reactions in patients with specific genetic markers.

- **Increased Drug Development Efficiency:** Drugs can be designed and tested for specific genetic profiles. Example: Cancer therapies are now developed for patients with exact genetic mutations, improving trial success rates and regulatory approval timelines.
- **Cost-Effectiveness in Healthcare:** The right drug, the first time, avoids unnecessary treatments and complications. Example: Pharmacogenetic testing reduces the cost of ineffective antidepressants by helping physicians choose a more likely match from the start.

Why This Matters for Trustees

Pharmacogenetics is not just a clinical tool, it's a cost-control mechanism and a strategic differentiator. Institutions that integrate it early can reduce adverse drug events, improve outcomes, and increase patient satisfaction.

Trustees should ask: Are we building infrastructure to support pharmacogenetic testing? Are providers trained to interpret genetic data? Are we integrating this data into our EHR systems?

The era of one-size-fits-all drug therapy is ending. Pharmacogenetics is the roadmap to what comes next.

Quiz Question

Which of the following is NOT an expected outcome of pharmacogenetics?

  A. The ability to prescribe the same medication and dosage to all patients, regardless of their genetic background
  B. Reducing the risk of adverse drug reactions by identifying genetic risk factors
  C. Enhancing the effectiveness of medications by tailoring them to individual genetic profiles
  D. Decreasing healthcare costs by optimizing medication selection and reducing ineffective treatments

Correct Answer: A

Pharmacogenetics is designed to avoid one-size-fits-all prescribing by using genetic information to personalize treatment.

Chapter 28
Population Health Management
Shifting from Sick Care to Smart Care

Population Health Management (PHM) is a strategic, data-driven approach to improving the health outcomes of defined patient populations. It's not just about treating individuals who show up sick, it's about managing the health of entire groups proactively.

PHM blends analytics, care coordination, risk stratification, and patient engagement to create a more efficient, preventive, and equitable healthcare system. It aims to keep people healthier, reduce unnecessary costs, and close gaps in care, especially for those most at risk.

Core Mechanisms Behind Population Health Management

PHM depends on a tightly integrated mix of data systems, predictive tools, and human-centered interventions.

- **Data Analytics:** Aggregates and analyzes health data to identify population trends and patient risks. Example: EHR data is used to find patients with uncontrolled diabetes and connect them to lifestyle coaching programs.
- **Risk Stratification:** Segments the population based on health risk to prioritize intervention. Example: Predictive models flag patients likely to be readmitted, triggering early outreach and support.
- **Care Coordination and Integration:** Connects all parts of the care team to create a seamless experience. Example: A cardiologist, primary care physician, and community nutritionist collaborate to manage a heart failure patient's care.
- **Patient Engagement and Self-Management:** Empowers patients with tools and support to manage their own health. Example: A mobile app gives patients access to health records, educational content, and daily symptom trackers.

Transformative Applications in Healthcare

PHM is transforming how care is delivered, how risk is managed, and how systems operate.

- **Improved Preventive Care:** Problems are addressed before they escalate. Example: Using local health data, clinics target flu vaccine efforts in ZIP codes with low historical uptake.

- **Enhanced Chronic Disease Management:** Integrated programs drive better long-term outcomes. Example: Patients with COPD receive personalized care plans including medication adherence support and in-home air quality monitoring.
- **Reduced Healthcare Costs:** Fewer avoidable ER visits and readmissions translate into financial sustainability. Example: A PHM initiative cuts asthma-related ER visits in half through proactive case management and patient education.
- **Health Equity:** PHM identifies and responds to care disparities. Example: Culturally tailored diabetes programs are deployed in communities with high prevalence and limited access to care.

Why This Matters for Trustees

PHM is not just a clinical strategy, it's an operational imperative. It improves quality scores, controls costs, and meets regulatory expectations around value-based care.

Trustees should ask: Are we investing in the right data infrastructure? Do we have aligned incentives for prevention, not just intervention? Are we engaging at-risk populations effectively?

Population Health Management is how health systems move from episodic care to continuous, coordinated health support, at scale.

Quiz Question

Which of the following is NOT a goal of population health management?

- A. Increasing the reliance on emergency care as the primary source of treatment
- B. Reducing the incidence and impact of chronic diseases in the population
- C. Enhancing the coordination of care among healthcare providers
- D. Improving patient engagement in their own health and wellness

Correct Answer: A

PHM focuses on prevention and early intervention, not sending more patients to the emergency department.

Chapter 29
Precision Medicine
Customizing Care for Every Patient

Precision medicine is transforming the one-size-fits-all model of healthcare. Instead of treating patients based on averages, it tailors prevention, diagnosis, and treatment strategies to the individual, using their genetic, environmental, and lifestyle data.

This approach allows clinicians to deliver more effective therapies, avoid harmful side effects, and proactively manage risk. It's not just personalization, it's prediction and prevention based on who the patient truly is, down to their DNA.

Core Mechanisms Behind Precision Medicine

Precision medicine relies on several integrated technologies and methods:

- **Genomic Sequencing:** Analyzes a patient's DNA to find mutations or variations that

influence disease and treatment response.
Example: Whole-genome sequencing identifies
a rare cancer mutation, guiding a patient
toward a targeted therapy that specifically
addresses that gene.

- **Biomarker Testing:** Measures biological
  indicators that help predict disease behavior
  and response to treatment. Example: Testing for
  HER2 in breast cancer determines whether a
  patient will benefit from HER2-targeted
  therapy.

- **Data Analytics and AI:** Uses advanced
  algorithms to analyze vast health datasets and
  generate personalized insights. Example: A
  machine learning model combines a patient's
  genetic profile, family history, and lifestyle to
  assess their risk for type 2 diabetes.

Transformative Applications in Healthcare

Precision medicine is already redefining how healthcare is
delivered, especially in high-stakes areas like oncology and
chronic disease.

- **Targeted Cancer Therapy:** Treatment is
  matched to the specific genetic mutations of the
  tumor. Example: A lung cancer patient receives
  a therapy that only targets cells with an ALK
  gene rearrangement, improving outcomes and
  sparing healthy tissue.

- **Personalized Drug Therapy:** Medications and dosages are chosen based on a person's metabolic profile. Example: Genetic testing reveals how a patient will metabolize antidepressants, guiding physicians to the safest and most effective option.
- **Risk Assessment and Prevention Strategies:** High-risk individuals are identified early and monitored more closely. Example: Genomic screening identifies a patient's risk for BRCA-related breast cancer, leading to earlier and more frequent screenings, or preventive surgery.
- **Chronic Disease Management:** Individualized treatment plans are built using precise, multi-dimensional data. Example: A personalized nutrition and fitness plan based on a patient's genetic markers helps manage prediabetes more effectively than generic advice.

Why This Matters for Trustees

Precision medicine represents the future of value-based care, where better outcomes are achieved through smarter, more targeted interventions. It also reduces unnecessary treatments, streamlines drug selection, and boosts patient satisfaction.

Trustees should evaluate: Are providers trained to interpret and act on genetic data? Is the EHR equipped to integrate genomic and lifestyle inputs? Are data privacy safeguards in place to protect sensitive personal health information?

Precision medicine is not just a clinical upgrade, it's a shift in how we define and deliver care.

Quiz Question

Which of the following is NOT a component of precision medicine?

    A. Developing universal treatment protocols that apply to all patients with a given disease

    B. Tailoring cancer therapy based on the genetic makeup of an individual's tumor

    C. Using pharmacogenomics to determine the most effective medication for a patient

    D. Implementing personalized prevention strategies based on genetic risk factors

Correct Answer: A

Precision medicine replaces universal protocols with targeted approaches based on each patient's unique profile.

Chapter 30
Predictive Analytics
Forecasting the Future of Healthcare

Predictive analytics in healthcare leverages historical data, statistical techniques, and machine learning to anticipate future outcomes. It helps providers shift from reactive to proactive care, identifying risks before they become emergencies, planning resources before they're depleted, and tailoring treatments before trial and error begins.

This isn't just about forecasting, it's about giving healthcare systems the ability to act earlier, smarter, and more efficiently.

Core Mechanisms Behind Predictive Analytics

Predictive analytics is powered by three main mechanisms:

- **Data Mining:** Finds patterns within massive datasets to inform future predictions. Example: Mining patient records reveals correlations between certain lab results and the onset of diabetes.

- **Machine Learning Models:** Use algorithms that improve with more data exposure. Example: A readmission prediction model flags patients at high risk of returning to the hospital within 30 days based on their discharge profile and prior outcomes.

- **Statistical Analysis:** Applies regression, probability, and trend analysis to healthcare variables. Example: Regression models predict the spread of influenza in a region using infection rates and travel data.

Each mechanism contributes to creating predictive tools that inform both individual treatment and system-level decisions.

Transformative Applications in Healthcare

The real impact of predictive analytics is seen in its applications across clinical and operational domains.

- **Enhanced Disease Management and Prevention:** Early warnings lead to early interventions. Example: A risk score identifies patients most likely to suffer heart failure within a year, prompting preemptive lifestyle counseling and medication.

- **Optimized Resource Allocation:** Anticipating demand improves efficiency. Example: Predictive models forecast ER traffic during flu season, guiding staffing decisions and vaccine distribution.
- **Personalized Patient Care:** Forecasts guide customized treatment plans. Example: Algorithms predict which cancer therapy is most likely to work based on a patient's unique genetic and clinical profile.
- **Improved Public Health Surveillance:** Detects outbreaks before they spread widely. Example: Real-time data and mobility tracking predict the next wave of COVID-19, enabling faster deployment of resources.

Why This Matters for Trustees

Predictive analytics transforms data into strategy. It improves care quality, reduces costs, and boosts operational resilience.

Trustees should ensure that analytics tools are transparent, evidence-based, and used ethically. Are clinicians trained to act on predictions? Are algorithms validated across diverse populations? Are privacy safeguards in place?

The better we predict, the better we prevent, and the better we perform as healthcare organizations.

Quiz Question

Which of the following is NOT a use case of predictive analytics in healthcare?

- A. Predicting patient no-shows to optimize appointment scheduling
- B. Forecasting the exact date a patient will develop a specific disease
- C. Identifying patients at risk of chronic diseases for early intervention
- D. Estimating future demands for hospital beds during flu season

Correct Answer: B

Predictive analytics estimates probabilities and risk, but not precise dates of disease onset.

Chapter 31
Quantum Computing
**Reshaping Healthcare Through
Quantum Speed and Scale**

Quantum computing is not an incremental advance, it's a foundational leap. It uses the principles of quantum mechanics to process data at speeds and depths that traditional computers cannot match. In healthcare, this means faster drug discovery, more powerful genomic analysis, and deeply personalized care built on vast, complex data.

Where classical computers evaluate possibilities one at a time, quantum systems explore many simultaneously. This parallelism enables a new class of problem-solving, especially in medicine, where complexity often exceeds current computing capacity.

Core Mechanisms Behind Quantum Computing

Quantum computing relies on three key quantum properties:

- **Quantum Bits (Qubits):** Qubits can exist in multiple states at once, unlike classical bits. Example: Analyzing thousands of genetic sequences at the same time to accelerate genome mapping and comparison.
- **Quantum Entanglement:** Entangled qubits are instantly linked, no matter the distance. Example: Comparing genomic data across large populations simultaneously to identify genetic markers for disease susceptibility.
- **Quantum Superposition:** Qubits can represent multiple outcomes at once, enabling faster problem-solving. Example: Exploring billions of molecular combinations for new drug candidates in seconds instead of years.

These properties allow quantum computers to solve problems that are currently computationally infeasible.

Transformative Applications in Healthcare

Quantum computing is poised to unlock new capabilities across several healthcare domains:

- **Accelerated Drug Discovery and Development:** Simulates molecular interactions at quantum precision. Example: A quantum model reveals how a protein folds and how a compound can bind to it, drastically shortening drug development cycles.

- **Enhanced Genomic Sequencing:** Speeds up genome analysis for faster diagnosis and risk prediction. Example: Sequencing a patient's genome in minutes instead of hours, enabling earlier intervention for genetic conditions.
- **Complex Data Analysis for Personalized Medicine:** Integrates and interprets massive, multidimensional datasets. Example: Simultaneously analyzing data from EHRs, wearables, and genetic tests to recommend custom treatment protocols.
- **Optimization of Healthcare Logistics:** Solves combinatorial problems faster and more efficiently. Example: A quantum algorithm determines the optimal use of hospital beds, staff schedules, and OR time to improve care delivery and reduce costs.

Why This Matters for Trustees

Quantum computing is not widely deployed yet, but it's advancing quickly. Healthcare systems should begin preparing now by investing in quantum-ready infrastructure and exploring early pilot programs.

Trustees should ask: Are we building partnerships with quantum research centers? Are our data systems capable of supporting quantum-scale analysis? Are our clinicians and IT teams beginning to understand the implications?

Quantum computing won't cure disease overnight. But

it will give us tools to understand, prevent, and treat illness in ways we've never been able to before.

Quiz Question

Which of the following is NOT a current or potential application of quantum computing in healthcare?

A. Instantaneously curing diseases through quantum manipulation
B. Accelerating the process of drug discovery and development
C. Enhancing the speed and accuracy of genomic sequencing
D. Improving the efficiency of healthcare logistics and resource allocation

Correct Answer: A

Quantum computing supports faster analysis and discovery, but it does not directly cure diseases on its own.

Chapter 32
Robotic Process Automation
Automating the Back Office of Healthcare

Robotic Process Automation (RP refers to the use of software "robots" to automate repetitive, rule-based administrative tasks across healthcare systems. Unlike physical robots, RPA tools work at the user interface level, clicking buttons, filling forms, logging into systems, just like a human would, but with greater speed, accuracy, and consistency.

RPA isn't about replacing clinicians. It's about liberating them, and administrative staff, from high-volume, low-value work, allowing people to focus on care, strategy, and innovation.

Core Mechanisms Behind Robotic Process Automation

RPA tools typically involve three primary technical capabilities:

- **Rule-Based Task Automation:** Executes routine steps based on logical rules and structured data. Example: An RPA bot extracts billing codes from a clinical document and enters them into a billing platform with no manual oversight.
- **System Integration Without APIs:** Works across legacy systems and newer platforms by mimicking user behavior. Example: A bot logs into multiple systems, an EHR, a claims portal, and a lab database, to compile patient records for audit preparation.
- **Workflow Orchestration:** Coordinates multiple bots or steps in a multi-system task sequence. Example: Upon patient discharge, RPA updates the EHR, sends follow-up reminders, closes billing loops, and triggers a satisfaction survey.

Transformative Applications in Healthcare

RPA is already being deployed across operational and clinical-adjacent workflows:

- **Revenue Cycle Management:** Speeds up claims processing, reduces denials, and improves cash flow. Example: Bots check claim status daily, resubmit rejections, and update the billing system automatically.

- **Prior Authorization and Eligibility Verification:** Automates what used to take hours of phone calls and portal logins. Example: A bot confirms coverage and submits authorization requests based on real-time payer requirements.
- **Patient Scheduling and Communications:** Reduces human error and improves access. Example: RPA scans appointment calendars, finds gaps, and sends reminders or rescheduling prompts to patients.
- **Clinical Data Abstraction and Reporting:** Extracts and compiles data for registries, audits, or quality reporting. Example: A bot identifies all diabetic patients without a recent A1C and populates a report for care teams.

Why This Matters for Trustees

RPA offers immediate, measurable ROI. It reduces operational costs, increases compliance, and minimizes burnout caused by data entry overload. Unlike large-scale IT overhauls, RPA is low-risk, modular, and fast to deploy.

Trustees should ask: Are we investing in labor-intensive processes that bots could handle? Are we scaling RPA alongside clinical analytics? Are our compliance and security teams overseeing RPA governance?

RPA doesn't eliminate jobs, it reassigns them from data shuffling to higher-value thinking. It's what lets hospitals do more with less, and do it faster.

Quiz Question

Which of the following is NOT a common application of Robotic Process Automation in healthcare?

- A. Automatically verifying insurance eligibility for scheduled appointments
- B. Performing complex medical diagnoses based on clinical imaging
- C. Extracting data for quality reporting from multiple systems
- D. Submitting claims and managing follow-up on rejected invoices

Correct Answer: B

RPA handles administrative tasks, not clinical interpretation. Medical diagnoses require AI tools or human oversight.

Chapter 33
Smart Hospitals
**Digitally Reengineering Healthcare
from the Inside Out**

Smart hospitals represent a new paradigm in healthcare, one where technology, data, and automation converge to enhance patient care, improve safety, and optimize operations. By embedding advanced technologies such as the Internet of Things (IoT), artificial intelligence (AI), machine learning, and big data analytics into their infrastructure, these facilities are redefining what's possible in modern medicine.

More than just high-tech buildings, smart hospitals are data-driven ecosystems that support continuous, personalized, and responsive care.

Core Mechanisms Behind Smart Hospitals

The smart hospital model depends on a tightly integrated digital foundation:

- **Internet of Things (IoT) Devices:** Sensors and connected medical equipment capture and transmit real-time data. Example: Wearables monitor heart rate and oxygen saturation, sending alerts to staff if levels exceed safe thresholds.
- **Artificial Intelligence and Machine Learning:** AI systems process data to support diagnostics, predict risks, and guide interventions. Example: An AI tool flags anomalies in chest X-rays, assisting radiologists in identifying pneumonia earlier.
- **Big Data Analytics:** Patterns from hospital operations and clinical outcomes are mined for actionable insights. Example: Analyzing historical admissions and discharge rates to optimize bed management and staff scheduling.
- **Digital Health Records and Integrated Care Platforms:** Unified systems ensure clinicians access the full patient story at every touchpoint. Example: A centralized EHR integrates lab results, imaging, and physician notes across departments and specialties.

Transformative Applications in Healthcare

Smart hospitals improve healthcare not just at the bedside, but at every layer of the system.

- **Enhanced Patient Monitoring and Safety:**
  Continuous, real-time surveillance enables fast
  responses to health deterioration. Example:
  Smart beds detect when a patient at fall risk
  attempts to get up, triggering an alert to nursing
  staff.
- **Operational Efficiency and Cost Reduction:**
  Automation reduces waste and frees up staff for
  higher-value work. Example: Inventory systems
  automatically reorder supplies when levels
  drop below threshold, avoiding stockouts and
  overstocking.
- **Improved Patient Experience and
  Engagement:** Digital tools empower patients to
  manage appointments, access records, and stay
  informed. Example: A patient logs into their
  mobile app to check lab results, schedule
  follow-ups, and message their doctor, all in one
  interface.
- **Data-Driven Decision Making and
  Personalized Care:** Analytics help clinicians
  tailor care to each patient's risk profile and
  history. Example: Predictive models flag
  patients at risk for sepsis hours before
  symptoms present, enabling preventive
  treatment.

Why This Matters for Trustees

Smart hospitals are a competitive advantage in today's healthcare economy. They improve outcomes, lower costs, and enhance the patient experience, all while positioning the organization for a tech-enabled future.

Trustees should consider: Are we investing in interoperable systems? Are our teams trained to use the tools we've deployed? Are data governance and cybersecurity frameworks keeping pace?

This isn't about chasing trends. It's about building the infrastructure to deliver safer, faster, smarter care, consistently.

Quiz Question

Which of the following is NOT a characteristic feature of smart hospitals?

- A. Manual record-keeping and patient monitoring without the use of digital tools
- B. Real-time health monitoring using IoT devices
- C. Automated inventory management systems
- D. Use of AI to analyze health data and support clinical decisions

Correct Answer: A

Manual systems are the opposite of what defines a smart hospital. Automation and digitization are core.

Chapter 34
Synthetic Data
**Enabling Innovation Without
Compromising Patient Privacy**

Synthetic data in healthcare refers to artificially generated datasets that replicate the statistical properties and structure of real patient data, but contain no identifiable personal information. These datasets are created using machine learning algorithms and simulation techniques to mimic real-world data scenarios without exposing sensitive information.

Synthetic data enables innovation in research, algorithm development, and system testing, without triggering the regulatory and ethical risks that come with real patient records.

Core Mechanisms Behind Synthetic Data

Synthetic data relies on advanced statistical and generative methods:

- **Data Modeling and Simulation:** Uses real data to train models that generate artificial datasets with similar patterns. Example: A machine learning model learns the relationships between lab values, diagnoses, and outcomes, then generates new, but fictional, patient records.
- **Differential Privacy Techniques:** Ensures the synthetic data cannot be reverse-engineered to identify real individuals. Example: A health system shares synthetic records with a vendor to train an AI tool, while maintaining compliance with HIPAA and privacy laws.
- **Generative Models (e.g., GANs):** Uses neural networks to generate high-fidelity synthetic data, especially for images or complex variables. Example: GANs create synthetic X-rays that resemble real ones, enabling radiology AI development without using protected health information.

Transformative Applications in Healthcare

Synthetic data is increasingly used across healthcare R&D, quality improvement, and software development.

- **AI and Algorithm Training:** Provides abundant, risk-free data for model development. Example: A health system trains an AI to detect cancer in mammograms using synthetic images that reflect real-world variability.

- **Software Testing and Development:** Simulates patient interactions and data flows without needing real data. Example: Developers test an EHR interface using synthetic patient profiles that mimic diverse use cases.

- **Research and Academic Collaboration:** Enables data sharing across institutions without privacy hurdles. Example: A university shares synthetic COVID-19 datasets with partner institutions for joint predictive modeling.

- **Data Augmentation for Rare Conditions:** Enhances underrepresented cases in datasets. Example: Synthetic data balances datasets by simulating cases of rare genetic disorders for better algorithm generalization.

Why This Matters for Trustees

Synthetic data accelerates innovation while protecting patient trust. It enables safe data sharing, faster experimentation, and broader collaboration, without breaching confidentiality.

Trustees should ask: Are we using synthetic data to support R&D while complying with privacy standards? Are we validating synthetic models to ensure they reflect real-world outcomes? Are we using this capability to close data gaps in AI development?

Synthetic data isn't a substitute for real patients, but it's a powerful rehearsal space where innovation can happen safely.

Quiz Question

Which of the following is NOT a benefit of using synthetic data in healthcare?

A. Enabling AI model training without exposing real patient information

B. Sharing detailed patient records across hospitals without consent

C. Simulating rare disease cases to improve algorithm accuracy

D. Testing software systems with no risk of HIPAA violations

Correct Answer: B

Synthetic data protects privacy. Sharing real patient records without consent violates compliance, regardless of the use case.

Chapter 35
Telemedicine
Expanding Access and Redefining Care Delivery

Telemedicine uses telecommunications technology to deliver healthcare remotely. Whether it's a video consultation with a specialist or continuous remote monitoring of vital signs, telemedicine brings care to the patient, rather than requiring the patient to go to care.

It's a game-changer for patients in rural areas, for people with mobility issues, and for health systems aiming to streamline services and reduce cost. Telemedicine isn't an alternative, it's now an integral part of modern healthcare delivery.

Core Mechanisms Behind Telemedicine

Telemedicine operates through several core modes of care delivery:

- **Real-Time Consultations:** Virtual visits via secure video allow doctors and patients to interact live. Example: A patient managing chronic hypertension has a virtual follow-up, during which the physician adjusts medication based on symptoms and readings.

- **Store-and-Forward:** Data is collected and sent for later review by a remote specialist. Example: A primary care physician uploads images of a suspicious mole; a dermatologist later reviews the files and provides a diagnosis.
- **Remote Patient Monitoring (RPM):** Data is collected continuously from patients and transmitted to healthcare teams. Example: A diabetic patient wears a glucose monitor that uploads data daily to their provider's dashboard for real-time tracking.

Transformative Applications in Healthcare

Telemedicine improves care access, reduces cost, and enhances patient engagement, all without compromising clinical quality.

- **Increased Access to Care:** Especially valuable for patients in underserved or rural areas. Example: A patient in a remote area has a neurology consult from a top specialist without leaving their county.
- **Enhanced Patient Engagement and Satisfaction:** Convenience encourages proactive participation in care. Example:

Patients manage their appointments, lab results, and messaging with providers through a secure mobile portal.

- **Cost-Effectiveness:** Saves on time, travel, and overhead. Example: A routine follow-up is conducted via video, saving both patient and provider the costs of an in-person appointment.
- **Improved Healthcare System Efficiency:** Optimizes the use of clinical resources and reduces unnecessary visits. Example: A virtual triage system screens minor symptoms and routes patients appropriately, keeping ERs clear for emergencies.

Why This Matters for Trustees

Telemedicine isn't just a short-term solution, it's a structural shift. Trustees must ensure their health systems are equipped with secure platforms, clinical protocols, and reimbursement strategies for virtual care.

Ask: Are we meeting patient expectations for digital access? Are we tracking telehealth outcomes as rigorously as in-person care? Are staff trained in both the technology and the bedside manner of virtual care?

Telemedicine expands your reach without expanding your footprint.

Quiz Question

Which of the following scenarios is NOT a typical use of telemedicine?

- A. A patient receives emergency surgery in a remote-operated robotic facility without any human medical staff present
- B. A patient in a rural area consults a specialist in a distant city via video conferencing
- C. A diabetic patient's glucose levels are monitored remotely, with data sent to their healthcare provider
- D. A dermatologist diagnoses skin conditions by reviewing images sent by the patient

Correct Answer: A

Emergency surgery requires direct clinical oversight. Telemedicine supports care, but doesn't replace critical human intervention in acute scenarios.

Chapter 36
Virtual Reality
Immersive Technology Transforming
Healthcare

Virtual Reality (VR) in healthcare enables immersive, interactive experiences that mimic real-world scenarios or create entirely new environments. Through the use of headsets and motion-tracking technologies, VR allows patients and professionals to engage with three-dimensional spaces in a highly controlled, responsive way.

It's not just about games or simulations, VR is now being used to manage pain, train surgeons, support rehabilitation, and improve patient education. The result is a more engaging, effective, and personalized approach to care and learning.

Core Mechanisms Behind Virtual Reality

Several core mechanisms drive the utility of VR in healthcare:

- **Immersive Simulation:** Fully virtual environments recreate real-world clinical or therapeutic scenarios. Example: A VR surgical simulation lets residents practice appendectomies in a risk-free, realistic setting.
- **Interactive 3D Modeling:** VR turns complex anatomy into interactive, explorable models. Example: Medical students can "walk through" a beating human heart to study its structure and function.
- **Pain Management and Rehabilitation:** Immersive environments can reduce pain perception and encourage therapeutic movement. Example: Burn patients are immersed in a snowy VR landscape during dressing changes, reducing pain without opioids.

Transformative Applications in Healthcare

VR's applications are rapidly expanding across clinical, educational, and psychological domains.

- **Enhanced Medical Training:** VR provides a repeatable, realistic environment to practice complex skills. Example: A neurosurgical trainee practices delicate procedures with haptic feedback, gaining experience without risk to a real patient.

- **Innovative Treatment Options:** VR is used in behavioral health to simulate scenarios that help patients process trauma or overcome phobias. Example: Veterans with PTSD participate in VR exposure therapy sessions designed to safely revisit combat environments.
- **Rehabilitation and Physical Therapy:** Engaging exercises in VR improve motivation and movement quality. Example: A stroke survivor plays a VR game that encourages use of an impaired limb, accelerating recovery.
- **Patient Education and Engagement:** VR makes complex medical information understandable. Example: A cardiologist uses a VR model to walk a patient through a planned stent procedure, reducing anxiety and improving informed consent.

Why This Matters for Trustees

VR is not a gimmick. It's a tool that improves clinical outcomes, enhances training, and increases patient engagement. It also has the potential to reduce costs by lowering medication use (like painkillers), reducing read-missions, and speeding up recovery.

Trustees should evaluate whether their organization is exploring VR applications aligned with clinical priorities. Are staff trained in VR deployment? Is there infrastructure for data integration and safety oversight? Are there opportunities to partner with VR developers for custom applications?

VR is not replacing healthcare professionals, it's equipping them with a more powerful way to teach, treat, and connect.

Quiz Question

Which of the following is NOT an application of VR in healthcare?

A. Performing actual surgeries remotely in real-time using VR equipment

B. Training medical students in surgical techniques in a virtual environment

C. Providing distraction therapy for patients undergoing painful procedures

D. Assisting in the rehabilitation of patients recovering from strokes

Correct Answer: A

Performing remote surgery falls under telemedicine and robotic surgery, not VR. VR supports training and therapy, not live procedures.

Chapter 37
Wearable Technology
Empowering Personal Health Through Continuous Monitoring

Wearable technology in healthcare refers to electronic devices worn on the body that track, analyze, and often transmit health-related data. What began as simple fitness trackers counting steps has evolved into advanced health monitors capable of tracking heart rhythms, sleep cycles, blood pressure, and even glucose levels in real time.

These devices bridge the gap between daily life and clinical care, putting health data directly into the hands of users while enabling healthcare providers to monitor patients remotely and more continuously than ever before.

Core Mechanisms Behind Wearable Technology

Three main systems power the health benefits of wearables:

- **Health Monitoring Sensors:** Collect
  continuous, real-time data on physiology and

activity. Example: A smartwatch tracks your heart rate during sleep and flags abnormalities like elevated resting heart rate or irregular rhythms.

- **Data Analysis and Feedback:** Mobile apps analyze the sensor data and return actionable insights. Example: A connected app reviews sleep trends and recommends bedtime adjustments or relaxation routines.
- **Telehealth Integration:** Some wearables send data directly to healthcare providers. Example: A wearable ECG device continuously monitors heart rhythms and sends alerts to a cardiologist if irregularities are detected.

Transformative Applications in Healthcare

Wearables are changing how healthcare is delivered, from prevention to chronic disease management.

- **Preventive Health Management:** Early warnings prompt early action. Example: A smartwatch detects a potential atrial fibrillation pattern and notifies the user to consult their doctor, possibly preventing a stroke.
- **Chronic Disease Management:** Real-time data supports ongoing treatment and lifestyle adjustments. Example: A diabetic patient uses a wearable glucose monitor that updates their

smartphone every five minutes with blood
sugar readings, allowing better insulin dosing.

- **Enhanced Patient Engagement:** Users are
more aware and involved in managing their
health. Example: A gamified fitness app
rewards users for hitting step goals,
encouraging consistent activity and lifestyle
changes.
- **Personalized Health Insights:** AI tools analyze
trends and make tailored recommendations.
Example: Based on combined sleep, heart rate,
and activity data, a wearable provides a daily
health score and personalized coaching
suggestions.

Why This Matters for Trustees

Wearables are more than gadgets, they're becoming essential tools in modern healthcare. They generate valuable
health data outside the clinic, encourage preventive care,
and facilitate remote management of chronic conditions.

Trustees should consider: Are wearables being integrated into our population health strategies? Are we
building systems that accept and interpret patient-gener-
ated data? Are we addressing data privacy and security as
wearables become more embedded in clinical workflows?

Wearable technology aligns with healthcare's move
toward personalization, prevention, and patient
empowerment.

Quiz Question

Which of the following is NOT a common feature of wearable technology in healthcare?

- A. Real-time tracking of physical activity and health metrics
- B. Automatic diagnosis of complex diseases without any clinical oversight
- C. Integration with mobile apps for data analysis and personalized feedback
- D. The ability to share health data with healthcare providers for remote monitoring

Correct Answer: B

Wearables provide health data and early alerts, but clinical diagnosis still requires trained medical professionals.

Chapter 38
Healthcare Technology Glossary

Ambient Clinical Intelligence

Passive AI systems that automatically document clinical conversations and structure EHR data.

Application Programming Interface (API)

A digital bridge that enables different software systems to exchange data seamlessly.

Artificial Intelligence (AI)

Technology that mimics human cognitive functions such as learning, reasoning, and decision-making.

Augmented Reality (AR)

Technology that overlays digital information onto the real world to enhance clinical visualization and training.

Big Data Analytics

Analyzing vast datasets to discover trends, optimize care, and guide healthcare decisions.

Biomarker Testing

Identifying biological indicators in blood, tissue, or fluids to detect disease or predict treatment response.

Care Coordination

The organized delivery of healthcare services across multiple providers and settings.

Chronic Disease Management Platform

A digital system that supports long-term care coordination and monitoring for conditions like diabetes or heart disease.

Clinical Decision Support System (CDSS)

A tool that analyzes data to help clinicians make informed decisions at the point of care.

Data Mining

Extracting patterns from large datasets to gain actionable insights.

Digital Front Door

A patient-centric digital access point that integrates scheduling, records, billing, and communications.

Digital Twin

A real-time virtual replica of a patient, device, or hospital system used for simulation and prediction.

Edge Computing

Processing healthcare data at the source (e.g., a device) rather than sending it to the cloud.

Electronic Health Record (EHR)

A digital version of a patient's paper chart used to manage health information over time.

Entity Recognition

NLP task that identifies specific information (e.g., drug names, diagnoses) in unstructured text.

Explainable AI (XAI)

AI systems designed to show how decisions are made, improving transparency and trust.

Federated Learning

A decentralized ML approach that trains models across institutions without sharing raw data.

Fast Healthcare Interoperability Resources (FHIR)

A healthcare-specific data standard that structures how patient information is shared between systems.

Genomic Sequencing

The process of analyzing a person's DNA to identify genetic variations for diagnosis or treatment.

Health Monitoring Sensors

Devices that continuously collect health and activity data from the body in real-time.

Healthcare Interoperability

The ability of different healthcare IT systems to exchange, interpret, and use data effectively.

Internet of Things (IoT)

A network of connected medical devices and sensors that share and analyze patient data in real time.

Liposomal Nanoparticles

Drug delivery systems that encapsulate medications to target specific cells while minimizing side effects.

Machine Learning (ML)

A branch of AI that enables computers to learn from data and improve over time without being explicitly programmed.

Medical Imaging AI

AI systems trained to detect abnormalities or support diagnostics in radiology, pathology, and beyond.

Natural Language Generation (NLG)

AI technology that converts structured data into human-like text for documentation or communication.

Natural Language Processing (NLP)

AI that enables computers to understand and derive meaning from human language.

Nanosensors

Microscopic sensors that detect molecular-level changes, often used in continuous health monitoring.

OAuth 2.0

A protocol that securely allows third-party applications to access user data with permission.

Personalized Medicine

Tailoring treatment to an individual based on genetic, environmental, and lifestyle data.

Pharmacogenetics

The study of how a person's genetic makeup affects their response to medications.

Population Health Management (PHM)

A strategy to improve health outcomes of groups through data analytics and coordinated care.

Predictive Analytics

The use of data, statistical models, and ML to forecast future outcomes and risks.

Quantum Computing

A computational approach using quantum mechanics to solve complex problems exponentially faster than classical computers.

Quantum Entanglement

A quantum state in which two particles are instantaneously linked, no matter the distance.

Quantum Superposition

The ability of quantum bits to exist in multiple states at once, allowing parallel computation.

Qubit

The basic unit of quantum computing, capable of holding multiple values simultaneously.

Remote Patient Monitoring (RPM)

Technology that tracks patient health data remotely and sends it to providers for review.

Risk Stratification

Categorizing patients by health risk to target interventions more effectively.

Robotic Process Automation (RP

Software bots that automate repetitive, rule-based administrative tasks in healthcare operations.

Sentiment Analysis

Using NLP to determine the emotional tone of patient feedback or communications.

Smart Hospital

A facility that integrates digital technologies like IoT, AI, and analytics to improve patient care and operations.

Smart Inhaler

A connected device that tracks medication usage and provides adherence data for respiratory care.

Store-and-Forward Telemedicine

The transmission of health data (e.g., images, reports) to a provider for later evaluation.

Supervised Learning

A type of ML where models are trained using labeled datasets to make predictions.

Synthetic Data

Artificially generated data that mimics real patient records without compromising privacy.

Telemedicine

The use of telecommunications technology to deliver healthcare services remotely.

Unsupervised Learning

ML that finds hidden patterns in data without predefined labels.

Virtual Reality (VR)

Immersive technology that simulates 3D environments for medical training, therapy, and patient education.

Virtual Triage

Automated systems that assess symptoms and route patients to appropriate care levels.

Wearable Technology

Devices worn on the body that collect real-time health and fitness data.

Workflow Orchestration

Automated coordination of multi-step processes across different systems or departments.

Chapter 39

Obscure Healthcare Tech Terms Trustees Might Encounter

21st Century Cures Act Final Rule

Federal legislation mandating data interoperability and patient access to health records via APIs.

Acoustic Biosensing

The use of sound waves to detect physiological changes, such as blood flow or respiratory rate.

Actigraphy

A non-invasive method of monitoring rest/activity cycles using wearable motion sensors.

Active Metadata Management

A system that automatically tags and tracks data usage, lineage, and relationships in real-time analytics environments.

AIOps (Artificial Intelligence for IT Operations)

The application of AI to automate and enhance IT system monitoring, performance tuning, and incident response.

Bioimpedance Analysis

A technology that estimates body composition (like fat and muscle mass) by measuring electrical impedance.

Blockchain-as-a-Service (BaaS)

Cloud-based solutions offering plug-and-play blockchain infrastructure for healthcare data integrity and audit trails.

Capsule Endoscopy

A diagnostic technique involving a swallowable, camera-equipped capsule that captures GI tract images.

ChatOps

A method of automating system operations through chat interfaces like Slack or Microsoft Teams.

Clinical Data Lake

A centralized repository that stores raw clinical data from multiple sources in its native format.

Clinical Ontology

A structured framework that defines relationships between medical concepts to enable semantic interoperability.

Closed-Loop Medication Administration

An automated system that confirms the five rights of medication delivery using barcodes and EHR integration.

Cognitive Load Indexing

A method for measuring clinician overload using biometric or behavioral tracking during EHR use.

Context-Aware Computing

Systems that use environmental and situational data to adapt content and functionality dynamically.

Cyber Hygiene

A set of baseline cybersecurity practices (like patching and access controls) required to maintain system health.

Digital Pathology

The acquisition, management, and interpretation of pathology information in a digital environment using whole slide imaging.

Digital Phenotyping

The use of data from smartphones and wearables to infer behavioral and mental health status.

Differential Privacy

A data anonymization technique that adds mathematical noise to protect individual identities in aggregated datasets.

Edge AI

Artificial intelligence deployed directly on local devices or sensors, eliminating reliance on cloud connectivity.

Elastic Compute

Cloud-based infrastructure that automatically scales computing resources up or down based on demand.

Federated Identity Management

A system allowing users to access multiple systems using one set of credentials across trusted domains.

Fuzzy Matching

An algorithmic approach to finding approximate rather than exact matches, useful in patient record deduplication.

Gait Analysis

The use of sensors or AI to evaluate the biomechanics of walking for fall risk or neurological diagnosis.

Graph Database

A type of database optimized for storing data with complex relationships, often used in clinical genomics.

Haptics

Technology that provides tactile feedback to simulate touch in VR/AR surgical training environments.

Health Information Mediator (HIM)

An architecture layer that orchestrates data exchange between health systems and applications in low-resource settings.

Homomorphic Encryption

A form of encryption that allows data to be analyzed or manipulated without being decrypted.

Human-in-the-Loop AI

A model in which human experts supervise, correct, or train AI systems during deployment.

Identity and Access Management (IAM)

A cybersecurity framework that controls who has access to digital healthcare systems and data.

Image Segmentation

AI technique that breaks medical images into regions for analysis, such as isolating tumors in radiology.

In Silico Trials

Simulated clinical trials conducted using computational models rather than human subjects.

Intent-Based Networking

A network management method where administrators define desired outcomes and the system automates configurations.

Interventional Informatics

The application of real-time informatics interventions directly into clinical workflows to guide decisions.

Knowledge Graph

A visual and relational map of interconnected clinical concepts, used for reasoning and decision support.

Latency-Sensitive Application

Software that requires immediate data response, often used in telemetry or robotic surgery.

Low-Code/No-Code Platforms

Software development tools that allow users to build applications without traditional programming.

Middleware

Software that connects different systems or applications, often used to integrate legacy hospital tech.

Multi-modal AI

AI that synthesizes multiple types of data, text, image, sound, for a more comprehensive clinical interpretation.

Nanorobotics

The theoretical use of nanoscale devices to perform precise medical interventions at the cellular level.

Near-Field Communication (NF

Short-range wireless technology used in patient ID wristbands, smart badges, or contactless check-in.

Neuroinformatics

An interdisciplinary field combining neuroscience and informatics to process brain imaging and cognitive data.

Optical Coherence Tomography (OCT)

A non-invasive imaging technique that captures 3D views of tissue microstructure, especially in ophthalmology.

Prescriptive Analytics

The use of data to not only predict outcomes but recommend specific actions to achieve optimal results.

Quantum Key Distribution (QK

A quantum-safe encryption technique ensuring secure transmission of health data in future networks.

Radiomics

The extraction of large amounts of quantitative features from medical images for precision diagnostics.

Redcap (Research Electronic Data Capture)

A secure web application used to collect and manage research and clinical trial data.

RISC-V in Medical Devices

An open-source chip architecture gaining popularity in medical device firmware for customizability and cost savings.

Self-Sovereign Identity (SSI)

A blockchain-based identity framework that lets patients control their digital identities and health data.

Smart Dust

Tiny wireless microelectromechanical sensors (MEMS) that can monitor environments or internal health indicators.

Zero Trust Architecture (ZT

A security model where no user or device is automatically trusted, even inside the network perimeter.

Afterword

How did I decide what terms to feature in this book?

It was a reasonably straightforward process. I gathered material from:

- roughly 80 academic papers dealing with hospital management
- publicly available, anonymized meeting minutes from hospital board meetings
- articles from Google with the keywords "trustee and hospital and technology" using a program called DevonAgent, which scoured the web for me every morning for 6 months at 5 AM.

I then put all of this material into DevonThink, the greatest research tool ever created, which assembled a concordance of the most frequently used terms in all this material. I then threw out the terms that didn't make any sense, or were out of context (i.e. Robert's Rules Of Order), and was left with about 35 terms that appeared to have the most significance.

I then used DevonThink again, with its AI plus a generative AI I trained, to parse the material and assemble it in the order it is presented.

Software tools I used to produce this book, in order:

- Emacs (org-mode) - planning/writing
- DevonAgent - daily research gathering
- Devon Think - organizing research
- MacWhisper - transcribing board meetings
- Hugging Face LLaMA - previz
- Vellum - book publishing

Translations of this book into Spanish, French, and German were completed using DeepL.

If I missed any terms you feel should be included, or if you spot any grammatical or spelling errors, please email me at books@rongalloway.com

If I use your suggestion, or you spot a mistake, I will credit you in the next edition. Bear in mind, I went to Georgia Tech, so English 'not my forte is.'

About The Series

The *Clear & To The Point* series was created for professionals, thinkers, and builders who want clarity, not clutter.

Each book is built on the principle that complexity can be explained without condescension, and that the best ideas need fewer words, not more.

We cut through jargon, abstractions, and management-speak to get to the real mechanisms that drive results.

Whether the subject is technology, health, strategy, or workflow, the focus is always the same: what works, why it matters, and how to use it.

Our goal is simple. Deliver insight that's operational, actionable, and built for people who are already busy.

Every volume in the series is well-researched, field-tested, and designed for professionals who need answers, not theory. If you want hype, there are plenty of other places to find it. If you want books that make sense on the first read, and hold up on the second, this series was built for you.

You can find the *Clear & To The Point* Series everywhere you order books online.

Visit us at www.clearandtothepoint.com

About the Author

I am Ron Galloway. I have been a researcher for 38 years. I am the author of several books in the "Clear & To The Point" series, and I have made several films. I have keynoted 600+ conferences.

I'm a graduate of Georgia Tech. I was an analyst at Robinson-Humphrey/American Express, then Smith Barney, then spent 10 years at an analytical RIA. In 2006 I started a research company, and have been happily reading since.

Odds & Ends: My documentary on WalMart was the first film ever to premiere in the US Capitol Building. For some reason, I made a film on the neuroscience of PowerPoint.

I speak at conferences and board meetings quite frequently. If you're interested in having me speak, please visit www.rongalloway.com

X x.com/rongalloway

Also by Ron Galloway

BOOKS: CLEAR & TO THE POINT SERIES

AI: Clear & To The Point

Tech Terms For Trustees

You, Multiplied

Data To Dignosis

Writing Business Books

FILMS

Why WalMart Works

Rethinking Powerpoint

Folly Island

Black Box Doc (Summer 2025)

F-WMD: Financial Weapons Of Mass Distruction (Fall 2025)

www.ingramcontent.com/pod-product-compliance
Lightning Source LLC
Chambersburg PA
CBHW041209220326
41597CB00030BA/5147